In the complex world of school, every teacher needs a rock, something to anchor their moment-by-moment decisions that profoundly impact each child's life. Peter Johnston's not-to-be-missed revised edition of *Choice Words* is that steadying rock. Setting this book apart from others, Peter clearly explains why embracing a mindset that develops the social-emotional alongside academics is an essential component of children's literacy learning, and, what happens when we don't. With many new and accessible examples, he demonstrates how to effortlessly weave a more conscious choice of language into one's practice that benefits all of our children. Peter's compelling new edition will change your professional life, (and maybe your personal life as well), now and forever.

—**Kathy Champeau**, Reading Specialist,
Literacy Consultant, Teacher and Child Advocate

When Peter writes, "Once we start noticing certain things, it is difficult not to notice them again," he is spot on. Once you read about the importance of teacher language you have a mental model for the rest of your life. In this powerful second edition of *Choice Words* Dr. Johnston makes an unforgettable connection between the way a teacher speaks and the mindsets that develop in their students. Whether you are new to *Choice Words* or have read it before, this second edition is a must-read.

—**Holly Prast**, Assistant Superintendent
for the Kimberly Area School District

Twenty years after the publication of Peter Johnston's seismic groundbreaker *Choice Words*, the language that teachers and their students use in classrooms continues to be a big deal! In this eagerly-awaited revision, Johnston guides new and seasoned readers to notice, name, and mull the significance of classroom language patterns that build agency, foster a growth mindset, and ultimately equip children to contribute to a just and democratic society. Indeed, "talk is the central tool of our trade," and with this text Johnston offers educators a transformative apprenticeship to his decades-long study of classroom interactions that fuel human growth. Updates include a strong emphasis on anti-bias, anti-racist

T0340890

teaching and social-emotional learning. Chapters end with practical "Extensions" for further learning and application.

—**Annie Ward**, Co-author of *From Striving to Thriving* and *Intervention Reinvention*

The first edition of *Choice Words* ranks at the top of my list of professional books for educators. Happily, the second edition continues to occupy that top spot. Although we sometimes wonder if we need a second edition of a book, I assure you that we need this one! Peter Johnston understands and illuminates the power of language in teaching and learning. Teaching is a great deal about what we say and what we do. But too often we focus only on the instructional moves and ignore the importance of language to transform children's lives both in and out of the classroom. Peter's deep dive into language is staggering. He listens attentively to kids as if looking through a kaleidoscope of language with its intricate, ever-changing patterns- its nuance, its precision, and its power. Although based on solid, longstanding research, this book is not merely theoretical. It is also extremely practical and easy for educators to use. This second edition of *Choice Words* is filled with ideas, approaches, and actions, all carefully rooted in thoughtful consideration of how to build capable, agentive children. My first read of *Choice Words* forever changed me as a teacher and even as a mom. I've loved it, and as with the first edition, I will return to this new edition time and time again. I'm hoping and guessing you will do the same. Enjoy!

—**Stephanie Harvey**, Author/Co-author of *Strategies That Work, From Striving to Thriving* and *The Comprehension Toolkit*

Choice Words

How Our Language Affects Children's Learning

SECOND EDITION

Peter Johnston

Foreword by P. David Pearson

Routledge
Taylor & Francis Group

NEW YORK AND LONDON

A Stenhouse Book

Second edition published 2024
by Routledge
605 Third Avenue, New York, NY 10158

and by Routledge
4 Park Square, Milton Park, Abingdon, Oxon, OX14 4RN

Routledge is an imprint of the Taylor & Francis Group, an informa business

First edition published by Stenhouse 2004

Credits:

Frontispiece: From "Sticks and Stones May Break My Bones" in *Herbs Poems: A Collection* by H.J. Warren. Copyright 1982 by Friends of H.J. Warren. Reprinted with permission of Archimedes Press, Rockport, Maine.

Pages 77–78: From *How's It Going?* by Carl Anderson. Copyright 2000 by Carl Anderson. Published by Heinemann, a division of Houghton Mifflin Harcourt, Portsmouth, NH. All rights reserved. Reprinted with permission.

Adapted excerpts, pp. 225–229 from *Journal of Educational Psychology*, 2001, 92: 223–233. Copyright 2001 by the American Psychology Association. Adapted with permission.

ISBN: 978-1-625-31647-9 (pbk)
ISBN: 978-1-032-68083-5 (ebk)

DOI: 10.4324/9781032680835

Typeset in ITC Galliard Pro
by KnowledgeWorks Global Ltd.

Printed and bound in the United States of America by Sheridan

Sticks and Stones May Break My Bones

"Sticks and stones may break my bones
But words could never hurt me."
And this I knew was surely true
And truth could not desert me.

But now I know it is not so.
I've changed the latter part;
For sticks and stones may break the bones
But words can break the heart.

Sticks and stones may break the bones
But leave the spirit whole,
But simple words can break the heart
Or silence crush the soul.

HERB WARREN

For all the wonderful teachers
who have allowed me to learn from them.

Contents

Foreword

Choice Words is a book about the power of words—for good and ill. Words always insinuate power, but they can also tame, share, or even cede power. Choosing words carefully is, at once, a challenge and a privilege, and the challenge and privilege are magnified for teachers. Because we are granted the authority to shape classroom talk, we also shape opportunities, identities, and futures for students entrusted to our care. Words are tools of "othering" and "belonging." They can push students to the periphery of a classroom community or invite them into the core. They can be tools of exclusion that set students apart (that's the othering) or tools of inclusion that promote that all-important personal agency and collective equity (that's the belonging).

Compared to the first edition of *Choice Words*, much has been preserved. The basic logic of the enterprise of choosing words well is intact. But Peter and the scores of teachers with whom he has worked provide more and richer examples to extend and enhance the range and nuance of the issues and insights addressed. More fuel to light our individual and collective fires around this important responsibility.

A personal note. As I read the second edition of Peter's book, I thought a lot about my own work across many years in promoting students' growth in comprehension and learning. Why? Because classroom talk has been the engine for enhancing both understanding and knowledge. And I wish I could turn the clock back fifty years to the early 1970s and start over. Why? We knew a lot about how to shape our conversations around the ideas we wanted to promote. What we were naive about was making sure that our classroom talk also promoted personal agency and collective equity of the sort described in *Choice Words*. I am pretty sure that the work would have been better in meeting both ethical and learning goals. I won't do that work, but someone surely will.

The first edition of *Choice Words* was an anomaly—a professional book that became a bestseller. It became popular because it hit a sympathetic chord among teachers who sensed that their classroom talk was not doing its job of promoting both equity and learning. I am certain that the second edition will hit even more chords and help even more teachers orchestrate healthy, vibrant, equitable classrooms where learning and agency walk hand in hand. Read the book, enjoy it, learn from it. Better yet, read and discuss it with like-minded colleagues with whom you can practice choosing words that promote a mutual sense of belonging.

P. David Pearson,
Evelyn Lois Corey Emeritus
Professor of Instructional Science,
Graduate School of Education,
University of California, Berkeley

Acknowledgments

This book has a long history. The first edition grew out of a project begun by Michael Pressley and Dick Allington to study "exemplary teachers" as part of the National Research Center on English Learning and Achievement (CELA). My collaboration with Dick already stretched back twenty-three years, so my debt to him is particularly extensive. I'm also indebted to the co-directors of CELA, Arthur Applebee (now, sadly, deceased) and Judith Langer, and their wonderful support staff—particularly Mary Murphy and Janet Angelis. Funding for the project was provided through CELA, by the Research and Development Centers Program (Grant No. R305A6005) as administered by the Office of Educational Research and Improvement (now Institute of Education Sciences), US Department of Education. I also owe thanks to the other CELA researchers who were part of the original project, including Gay Ivey, Leslie Morrow, Ruth Wharton-McDonald, Nancy Farnan, Marcie Cox, Helen Foster James, along with (at the time) research assistants Kim Boothroyd, Greg Brooks, Melissa Cedeno, John Cronin, Jeni Pollack Day, Susan Leyden, Steven Powers, Jean Veltema, and Haley Woodside-Jiron. I also owe thanks to the teachers in that research, particularly Joan Backer, and Tracy Bennett.

I cannot thank enough the wonderful teachers who let my colleagues and me into their classrooms to document their teaching practice. Since the first edition of the book, I have spent considerable time learning from the following teachers: Susie Althoff, Jeralyn Johnson, Pegeen Jensen, Andrea Hartwig, Sarah Helmer, Merry Komar, Tara Krueger, Laurie McCarthy, Brian Lundstrom, and Amy Faulkner. Each of these teachers and their students showed me a different face and voice of the genius of teaching. I hope that this book does some justice to their remarkable daily work.

For the first edition of the book and into the intervening twenty years, I had a wonderful group of colleagues at The University at Albany, Jim Collins, Cheryl Dozier, KaiLonnie Dunsmore, Barbara Gioia, Ginny Goatley, Mark Jury, George Kamberelis, Becky Rogers, Donna Scanlon, Margi Sheehy, Sean Walmsley, and Rose Marie Weber. Along with Mary Unser (now, sadly, deceased) and Linda Papa, they sustained my work. Since I retired from the university, my colleagues have principally been Kathy Champeau and Gay Ivey, to each of whom I owe an enormous debt. I also owe intellectual debts to Marie Clay, Maria Nichols, and Katie Wood Ray.

I have quoted quite a bit of material in this book and I appreciate the consideration of the publishers who gave me permission to do so, including: The American Psychological Association, Guilford Press, Heinemann, Stenhouse, and Teachers College Press. I particularly appreciate the permission to reprint the poem by Herb Warren that appears as a frontispiece. If you would like to read more of his wonderful poetry, the book *Herb's Poems* is available only from the Friends of H.J. Warren at Box 399, Camden Maine, 04843.

The staff at Stenhouse (now also Routledge) have provided all kinds of support over the years, starting with Philippa Stratton who originally decided to publish *Choice Words* because, even though she doubted it would sell, she felt it should be published. For this edition, I owe thanks to Bill Varner, who bugged me to write a second edition, Kassia Wedekind who was my editor, Stefani Roth and Tom Bedford. And an anonymous reviewer.

Throughout the writing, I have been sustained, as ever, by my family, Tina, Nicholas, Emily, and Samantha. To them I must apologize for my frequent failures to engage them through language I know to be most helpful. I hope they forgive this frailty.

Preface to the Second Edition

Since the publication of the first edition of *Choice Words*, twenty years ago, there have been developments not only in research, but also in my experiences in excellent classrooms. With Maria Nichols, I spent time in the elementary classrooms of Susie Althof and Jeralyn Johnson. Those teachers, along with others such as Pegeen Jensen, led to my book *Opening Minds: Using Language to Change Lives*. Subsequently, Gay Ivey and I studied engaged reading in middle school, resulting in the book *Teens Choosing to Read: Fostering Social, Emotional, and Intellectual Growth Through Books*. Over the years, I spent considerable time in the elementary classrooms of Kathy Champeau, Andrea Hartwig, Sarah Helmer, Merry Komar, Tara Krueger and Laurie McCarthy, my co-authors of the book *Engaging Literate Minds: Developing Children's Social, Emotional, and Intellectual Lives, K-3*.

This edition of the book has been influenced by all of these experiences. I revised and updated existing chapters, preserving the parts of the book that have stood the test of time, and replaced less-compelling examples. I devoted more attention to the socio-emotional life of the classroom, a domain that now has its own chapter. The nature and significance of mindsets also earned its own chapter, and along the way I explore the biases that infect our language.

In the years since *Choice Words* was first published, many teachers have read and engaged with the ideas within the pages of this short book. Teachers have read it on their own, in book clubs, and in university courses. They have taken up the work, innovating and making it their own in ways that teachers tend to do so brilliantly. It is my hope that this new edition provides the space to do the same, for both readers familiar with *Choice Words* and those who read it for the first time.

CHAPTER 1

The Language of Influence in Teaching

It makes me think more educated in my mind when I read because of how Ms. Tucker talks to me.

Eighth grader Deandra[1]

When I was in fourth grade, in response to one of my transgressions, my teacher turned to me and said with relish, "By the gods thou art a scurvy knave. Verily I shall bonce thee on thy evil sconce." An observer might have chuckled and forgotten this brief and trivial event. Its genius is easily missed. His playful use of language simultaneously got my attention, stopping the inappropriate behavior, took the edge off the rebuke by making it playful, leaving my dignity intact (showing that he cared), and showed me how valuable and interesting language can be—valuable enough to play with, powerful enough to change behavior without force. He also showed the possibilities for adopting other voices, drawing language from other sources, while incidentally reminding us of a topic we had studied in social studies. It would be foolish to argue that this single event is the reason I use language as I do in my learning, thinking, teaching, and social life. Less foolish, I think, to point to it as an example of a conversational current that left its mark on my social and intellectual being. As with most of the teachers it has been my privilege to study, I doubt that my fourth-grade teacher was aware of the implications of his use of language. He was just good at using it in ways that assisted our learning. Some of us have to think more carefully about the language we use to offer students our best learning environment.

If we have learned anything from Lev Vygotsky it is that "children grow into the intellectual life around them."[2] That intellectual life is fundamentally social, and language has a special place in it. Because the intellectual life is social, it's also relational and emotional. The most humbling part of observing accomplished teachers is seeing the subtle ways they build emotionally and relationally healthy learning communities—intellectual environments that produce not mere technical competence, but caring, secure, actively literate human beings. Research shows that these achievements are not at odds. Quite the reverse, in fact.

Some years ago, I had read Mary Rose O'Reilly's *The Peaceable Classroom.* Early in the book she observes: "I had gone off to be a teacher, asking myself from time to time if it might be possible to teach English in such a way that people would stop killing each other."[3] Her confession reminded me of my own journey into teaching. I filed both under youthful idealism. I now realize I was wrong. It's both realistic and essential. In one classroom, in our original research, I noticed a student return from the library with a book. His teacher asked if he found the book he needed for his project. His cheerful answer? "Not yet, but I found one for Richard." In another school, I watched a class of fourth graders engage in a deeply philosophical discussion of science and ethics for an hour and a quarter with little input from the teacher. In another, over the course of four months, a student, who had been classified as emotionally disturbed, became behaviorally indistinguishable from his peers with none of his former outbursts. In the face of relentless testing pressures, these teachers accomplished some of what Mary Rose O'Reilly imagined—not without struggle, and not without soliciting the help of their students.

Exploring the nature of these teachers' skill, I have been particularly influenced by what children have to say. My colleague

Rose Marie Weber says that as a graduate student at Cornell she was introduced to some first graders. One of the girls commented that her father was going to be a doctor of philosophy. The teacher observed that Rose was too. The girl pointed out that Rose couldn't be a doctor of philosophy, she would have to be a nurse of philosophy. This first grader couldn't imagine herself becoming a doctor. Doubtless, she also could not imagine her brother becoming a nurse. She didn't make this up out of nothing. She made it up out of the discursive environment in which she was immersed. Despite protestations, we all carry such biases with us because they are embedded in the cultural discourse in which we are steeped.

Children teach us about the language of our classrooms. We have to ask what discursive histories make it possible for them to say what they say. What makes it possible for a student asked "Who else would like that book?" to respond, "Probably Patrick... He's, he's not the kind of guy who laughs, and he doesn't smile too much. And in this book, he might smile."[4] Why does another student describe herself as, "I'm on one of the lowest levels in this class. It really stinks... Most of them [classmates] are above me... I have Peter Williams and he doesn't care if I read with him and he always helps me out and stuff." How come a student in a different class distinguishes herself as a reader with, "I love to read mystery, adventure, suspense, and I like to read books about animals doing everyday things that we do... Barry likes to read about sports. And Amy likes to read about horses and dolphins... Amanda's reading is very different from mine because hers usually have a happy ending. Mine are like never-ending stories."[5] What classroom conversations lead to a student reporting that, "[recently] I have learned how to pronounce more words... How to read more faster than before... [and] I'd like to learn, how to pronounce more words"?[6] These children have a different sense of who they are and what they are doing. Teachers play a critical role in arranging the discursive histories from which these children speak. Talk is the central tool of our trade. It changes who people think they are and what they think they are doing.

If you think that what we think we're doing is no big deal, consider this. Alia Crum and Ellen Langer reframed the work of female hotel room cleaning staff by explaining that their work was actually excellent exercise.[7] Using examples, they showed how the

3

work met the Surgeon General's recommendations for an active lifestyle. A month later, this group who thought their work was good exercise felt they were getting more exercise than before. Because of that perception, their weight, body fat, body mass index, waist-to-hip ratio, and blood pressure had all dropped. They actually became healthier. Those whose work had not been reframed as exercise experienced no such benefits. I am confident that children's understandings of what they think they are doing are just as powerful.

Making Meaning: Making People

When parents interact with their baby, they *make* something meaningful out of what the baby "says." The fact that there is not much to work with doesn't stop them from constructing a conversation. From "bem ba" they impute a social intention and respond to it, "You want milk?" They act as if the baby's noises are not random but are intentional actions, and respond accordingly. Relationally they position the baby as a sentient, social being—a conversation partner. In the process, parent and child jointly construct the baby's linguistic and social development and lay the foundation for future interactions with others—how the baby expects to be treated and to interact.[8]

The same is true, in a way, in the classroom. Teachers have to make something of what children say and do. They make sense for themselves, and offer a meaning for their students. They impute intentions and offer possible worlds, positions, and identities. For example, suppose an independent book discussion group has deteriorated to chaos. The teacher decides to say something to the students. What does she say? Perhaps she says, "That group, get back to work or you'll be staying in at lunch." On the other hand, she might say, "When you are loud like that, it interferes with the other discussion groups and it makes me feel frustrated." On the other hand (yes, teachers have more than two hands), she might say, "This is not like you. What's the problem you've encountered? Okay, how can you solve it?" Each of these responses offers a different answer to "What are we are doing here?" "Who are we?" "How do we relate to one another in this kind of activity?" and "How do we relate to the object of study?" Each different

Table 1.1 Implications of Different Teacher Responses to Social Transgression

Teacher Comment **Question Answered by Comment**	That group, get back to work or you'll be staying in at lunch.	When you are loud like that, it interferes with the other discussion groups and it makes me feel frustrated.	This is not like you. What is the problem you have encountered? ... Okay, how can you solve it?
What are we doing here?	Laboring.	Living in cooperation.	Living collaboratively.
Who are we?	People who value compliance over agency.	People who care about others' feelings.	Social problem-solvers.
How do we relate to one another?	Authoritarian control.	Respectful with equal rights.	Work out our problems.
How do we relate to what we are studying?	Do it only under duress.	[no implication]	[no implication]

response has the potential to alter the subsequent interactions in the class. The implications of these options are unpacked a bit in Table 1.1.

In other words, language has "content," but it also bears information about the speaker and how they view the listener and their assumed relationship. Michael Halliday calls these the *ideational* and the *interpersonal* dimensions.[9] There is always an implicit invitation to participate in a particular kind of activity or conversation. We cannot persistently ask questions of children without becoming the one-who-asks-questions and placing children in the position of the one-who-answers-(and doesn't ask) questions.

Explicitness

Although language has its impact in many ways, a common focus of attention has been on the explicitness of the language teachers use.[10] Of course, if students need to know something, they shouldn't be reduced to guessing by their teacher's assumptions about what they "should" already know. There is no doubt that we often assume students know things, or know them in particular ways, when they do not. We ask kindergarteners, "What is the sound of the letter at the end of the word," forgetting that many of them are unclear about the concepts *letter*, *word*, *sound* (as it applies to speech), and *end* (which requires knowing that letters are ordered left to right), and do not know that letters bear a complex relationship to speech sounds.[11] As Margaret Donaldson notes in *Children's Minds*, "the better you know something, the more risk there is of behaving egocentrically in relation to your knowledge. Thus, the greater the gap between teacher and learner, the harder teaching becomes…"[12] That is, unless the teacher is able to imagine the child's perspective, a critical skill for responsive teaching.

People who come from different cultural backgrounds often encounter difficulties in their interactions. I once attended an Indian wedding. Among other blunders, as I proceeded down the reception line, I tried to shake hands with the women in the wedding party, which put them in a difficult position. Such experiences of being in a cultural minority are very good for reminding us that the ways people do things can be very different. It's especially easy for teachers from the dominant culture not to notice how difficult it can be for students from a different culture to figure out how things are done here. Those of us in the dominant culture are so used to not having to face such conflicts that we come to assume that everyone says and does things the way we do. Consequently, we don't explicitly detail how we do things because one of the rules of conversation is that you don't tell people what they already know.[13] Students whose color, class, or culture differs from their teacher's, the majority of whom are white and middle class, often pay a high price for this assumption, particularly those from historically marginalized cultures.

In other words, it's true that we are often less explicit than we might be, that we are confusing sometimes when we try to be explicit, and that being more thoughtfully explicit can be important. Nonetheless, there are many complications to explicitness. We can't be explicit about everything. The rules of conversation require limiting our explicit comments to what our partner doesn't already know and to what they might find interesting.[14] This means that deciding what to be explicit about requires some knowledge of our audience—and responsive teachers do have that knowledge of their students.[15]

The assumption that just being more explicit will make for better instruction assumes that language is simply a delivery system for information, a literal packaging of knowledge. It's not. Each utterance in a social interaction does much more work. For example, there are hidden costs in telling people things. If students can figure something out for themselves, to explicitly provide the information pre-empts the student's opportunity to build a sense of agency and independence, which, in turn, affects the relationship between teacher and student. Think about it. When you figure something out for yourself, there is a certain thrill in the figuring. After a few successful figuring out experiences, you might start to think that figuring things out is something that you actually can do. Maybe you're even a figuring-out kind of person, encouraging an agentive dimension to identity. When you're told what to do, particularly without asking, it feels different. Being told explicitly what to do and how to do it—over and over again—provides the foundation for a different set of feelings and a different story about what we can and can't do, and who we are. The interpretation might be that you are the kind of person who cannot figure things out for yourself. This is doubtless one reason why research has shown that most accomplished teachers do not spend a lot of time in telling mode, and that dialogic instruction is a more powerful option than direct instruction.[16]

As teachers we have to decide *what* to be explicit about for *which* students, and *when* to be explicit about it. Often, as anyone with teenagers knows, being explicit can be the perfect way to meet resistance. The back door is frequently more effective than the front. And, of course, explicitness doesn't account for some very powerful learning. Very little of our sense of masculinity and femininity,[17] for example, comes about through explicit instruction in the relevant behaviors, feelings, and values. Our involvements in gendered social-linguistic interactions have much more impact.[18] Of course,

7

in some situations, such as when physical harm is involved, our language must be thoroughly direct and explicit. I will try (explicitly?) to untangle some of these details in our conversations throughout this book.

Speech Is Action

Speaking is as much an action as hitting someone with a stick, or hugging them.[19] A minister, priest, rabbi, or imam, by pronouncing two people married, makes it so (to a point). We invite kindergarten students to make books, and treat their efforts exactly as we would those of the commercial authors they admire, inviting them to add "about the author" pages. We point out how "You put your name on the cover, just like Eric Carle did." Pretty soon, the children respond as authors. They notice the things authors notice and make the kind of decisions authors make, initiating making books the way commercial authors do.

Language, then, is not merely *representational* (though it is that), it's also *constitutive*. It actually creates realities and invites identities. Saying "You're so smart" to a child is very different from saying "You are so thoughtful." The phrases offer different views of what is valued and how peers might view and interact with the child. For the child, the phrases help answer the questions "Who am I?" and "How does a person like me act?"

Language works to *position* people in relation to one another.[20] For example, a teacher might position themselves as the giver of knowledge in the classroom, with the students as receivers of knowledge. A classic (and ubiquitous) example of this is the sequence in which a teacher asks a question to which they already know the answer, a child answers it and the teacher announces whether or not the child is correct. Teachers can position children as competitors or collaborators, and themselves as referees, resources, judges, or many other arrangements. A teacher's choice of words, phrases, metaphors, and interactions invokes and assumes these and other ways of being a self and of being together in the classroom.

Similarly, the way a teacher talks can position students differently in relation to what they are doing, learning, or studying. Talking about reading as "work" has different implications from referring

to it as "fun," or "an interesting new challenge." Consider this: Ellen Langer and her colleagues had people sorting cartoons as to
how humorous they were—basically a fun activity.[21] But the activity was referred to as "work" for half of the people and "fun" for
the other half. The "work" people did not enjoy the activity and
reported that their minds wandered while doing it. Similarly, telling
children they can have free choice time, "but first we have to finish
our reading," positions reading poorly simply by using the words
"have to."

Although language operates within relationships, language practices also influence relationships among people and, consequently,
the ways they think about themselves and each other. Language
even structures our perception—the sense we make of the neural
impulses that come to our brain from our sense organs and how we
experience emotions.[22] As Rom Harre and Grant Gillet point out,
"discourse penetrates a fair way into the perceptual system."[23] Just
as we actively seek sensory information to inform our construction
of reality, we actively seek new information to inform the narrative
we are building about who we are, and to ensure its genuineness.

In other words, the language teachers (and their students) use
in classrooms is a big deal. My intention with this book is to examine some of the ways in which it is a big deal by exploring words
and phrases that turn up in interactions between teachers and their
students. These words and phrases exert considerable power over
classroom conversations, and thus over students' literate, intellectual, social, and emotional development. In the rest of the book, I
list various language segments used (or systematically not used) by
teachers and explain briefly why I think they are significant. I have
clustered the words and phrases in what I hope are conceptually
useful categories, even though some of them will clearly belong in
multiple categories. Although these are mere fragments of interactions, I think of them as representative examples of linguistic families, in the sense that, though they have different surface forms, they
share some common features and common sociolinguistic genetic
material.[24]

My explanations of the significance of these language examples
will draw on a range of related disciplines. I assume that each conversational exchange between teacher and student(s) provides building
material for children's understanding of a range of literate concepts,
practices, and possibilities, and helps shape their identities, as each

exchange "becomes a fragment of autobiography."[25] Readers familiar with linguistics will realize that, from the get-go, I will take many liberties. For example, I will treat these language fragments as if we can make sense of them outside of the immediate context of their use. Of course, we can't. I will try to redeem myself along the way, particularly at the end of the book. In the meantime, I ask that you humor me. (If you are not inclined to humor me, please go to Appendix A for a little more explanation.)

Noticing and Naming

> Language is the essential condition of knowing, the process by which experience becomes knowledge.
>
> Michael Halliday[1]

The more people notice about something, the more they tend to like it. Ellen Langer and her colleagues had people engage in activities they didn't like such as watching football or listening to classical music or rap. However, some were asked to notice three, six, or nine new things about the activity. The more they noticed, the more they ended up liking it.[2] This is one reason we ask children "What are you noticing?" to encourage them to notice new things. Their noticing of new things has the added benefit of offering them agency in the teaching–learning relationship. They *initiate* the learning. Noticing new things is a big deal. It's at the heart of mindfulness.[3]

Having noticed something, we want to name it. Babies go through a "Wazzis?" (What's this?) stage when they discover that things have consistent names (of course they're also learning how to take control of social interactions by asking questions—and learning the fun of doing so). Noticing and naming is a central part of being a communicating human being, but it's also crucial to becoming competent in an activity. Becoming a physician requires learning what signs to notice, what to name particular clusters of signs, how to distinguish one drug from another, and how different drugs relate to different patterns of signs. Becoming a teacher requires knowing how to tell when learning is going well and when it's not, what children's sound spelling indicates about what they know, what it means when a child doesn't participate productively, and so forth—what to notice. As teachers we socialize children's attention to the significant features of literacy, math, or other domains, and we solicit their help by inviting them to notice new features and patterns.

Once we start noticing certain things it's difficult not to notice them again, the knowledge actually influences our perceptual systems.[4] And there are different ways of naming the same thing. Different schools of healing notice different features and give symptoms different significance. Different schools of teaching do the same. Two teachers with different frameworks of teaching have different names for when a child spells unconventionally. Feelings, too, are noticed and named. Our bodies respond to events, and in our interactions with others in our culture we learn which to attend to and what to call them—what sense to make of them—and whether they are something that we should talk about or not.[5] With our assistance, children are expanding and learning to manage their own attention, and the attention system is in many ways a "gatekeeper of knowledge acquisition."[6] For this reason we particularly want them to notice language and its significance.

Learning what things to notice and what to name them is a central part of apprenticeship, but we also learn things without naming them or even being aware of them. Language is the perfect example. We acquire language and by the time we arrive at school, we have remarkable facility with it. At the same time, we are largely unaware of it. It's not that children have no awareness. They've been able to lie and tell jokes for some time, which means that they know that with language they can consciously make something different from reality. However, many graduate high school with little change in their awareness, leaving them unprepared to manage the effects language has on them and on others. This leaves them at the mercy of advertisers, politicians, authors, and so forth. It also leaves them unaware of the effects their discursive histories have had on them. Failure to understand these relationships means that they cannot take up issues of social justice perpetuated through language. It's our responsibility to help children notice these things. The more they notice and bring to the class's attention the better, and the less the teacher needs to wear the mantle of the one-who-says-what's-important.

From here on in the book, I will unpack examples of teachers' talk, showing what I believe to be their impact on individual students and classroom communities. The examples of teacher talk appear as subheadings followed by an analysis of their significance.

❧ *"You can teach yourself to do lots of things. All you have to do is be a noticer. We'll notice lots of things this year and help each other to notice as well. You'll help me notice more too."* Laurie McCarthy tells her first and second graders this on the first day of school, deputizing them as collaborative curriculum developers. Throughout the year, she extends this thread by asking, "What are you noticing?" Remember? The more they notice about something, the more interesting they find it. When students notice something and bring it to the class's attention, they're exercising curricular agency, taking control of their learning lives, particularly if their noticing leads to even a micro lesson arising from the observation. We can help them with comments like, "When you noticed those words both have the same pattern, that helped us read all of these other words too." Highlighting the value of the children's noticings for their collective knowledge building will also build their sense of competence and agency, as will an acknowledgement that, "I didn't notice that until Rosa pointed it out," implying, "I just learned from Rosa," establishing Rosa as a bona fide knowledge contributor.

We also help children see what kind of things might be noticed: Did anyone *notice:* ... Any interesting words? ... any new punctuation? ... any words that are a bit alike? ... any new ways of arranging words on the page? Children can also benefit from invitations to notice their own behavior, as in: Did anyone *try:* ... Some new words they liked? ... some new punctuation? ... a different kind of writing? ... a different kind of reading? Did anyone: ... Create a new character? The idea in such questions is to normalize the practice of trying out new possibilities—stretching beyond what one already controls. To notice—to become aware of—the possible things to observe about the literate world, about oneself, and about others, can open conversations among students who are noticing different things.

❧ *"I see you know how to spell the beginning of that word."* When a child has spelled *farm* as *fm*, what is to be said? The most important piece is to confirm what has been successful (so it will be repeated) and simultaneously assert the growing competence of the learner so they will have confidence to consider new learning. Marie Clay referred to this as attending to the "partially correct."[8] Its significance cannot be overstated.

Focusing on the positive is hardly a new idea, it's just hard to remember to do it sometimes, particularly when the child's response is nowhere near what you *expected*. Indeed, the more we rely on expectations and standards, the harder it is to focus on what is going well. I recall being asked once what third graders' spelling *should* be like and wondering how knowing that might help or (more likely) hinder someone's teaching. Certainly, teaching to normative expectations will mean lots of positive feedback for some students (but not necessarily any new learning) and lots of negative feedback for others. Much more important is noticing—and helping the students to notice—what they are doing well, particularly the leading edge of what is going well. This leading edge is where the student has reached beyond herself stretching what she knows just beyond its limit, producing something that is partly correct. This is the launching pad for new learning, and recognizing it provides the energy to face the next challenge.

Noticing *first* the part that is correct, or makes sense, is a perceptual bias we need to extend to students. For example, if we ask a student to find any words that are not quite right in their writing and then to mark the part of the word that *is* right, we can ask them to explore other ways of spelling the not-quite-right piece, focusing on the problem to be solved. We can apply the same principle to a wide range of social and literate practices, such as analyzing group learning processes (as we shall see). I can't overemphasize the importance of this practice. Children with a solid sense of well-being are less likely to tell self-stories containing references to negative consequences or negative feelings.[9] Socializing children's attention to where and how they are being successful is also likely to develop their sense of self-efficacy[10] or agency (see Chapter 4).

❦ *"I want you to tell me how it [group discussion] went... What went well? ... What kinds of questions [were raised]?"*[11]

Here, Tracy Bennett was drawing students' attention to the process of group discussion, which, as we shall see in Chapter 8, is critical for both managing and arranging for productive learning communities. Second, asking what went well draws attention first to the productive aspects of the process to reinforce a solid foundation and build a productive community learning identity. Reviewing the experience as a positive narrative about the group process also builds an affinity for this sort of experience. Third, Tracy has drawn attention to the idea that there are different kinds of questions, just as there are different kinds of text, different kinds of writer, different kinds of words, and so forth. Noticing and talking about them is an important part of being a literate person.

🌱 *"Are there any favorite words or phrases, or ones you wish you had written?"*
This request at once turns children's attention to the qualities of words while implying (insisting, actually) that they all (obviously) want to write wonderful words—to be authors. It opens the possibility that they might be able to write such words, particularly if teachers notice choice words in children's writing or speech. For example, "I notice that your lead is like Doug Salati's lead in *Hot Dog*," names the concept of lead and shows that it's something that other, perhaps more renowned authors do. It opens the possibility of subsequent conversations about leads and using other authors' leads as resources.

On another occasion, after rereading a sentence in a read-aloud, the same teacher said, "Oh I love that line."[12] With this comment she does what she asks her students to do. She continues socializing their attention to language, opening it up for analysis, while also expressing an emotional response to the language. Studies of teaching often mistakenly neglect teachers' emotional responses. But even babies use the emotional indicators of their social partner as an important source of information about the environment.[13] Although loving the line is a verbal expression of an emotional response, all interactions are laden with affect and children attend to these expressions as much as to any other source of information. We must take seriously our attitudes toward particular children and domains of learning, maybe noticing more things about them.

🌱 *"What are you noticing? … Any other patterns or things that surprise you?"*[14]
In Joan Backer's fourth-grade class at the beginning of each day, a student (or some students, or Joan) picked out a word for the day

and wrote it up along with its meaning and diacritical markings—words such as "quagmire." Early in the afternoon, she covered it up and asked the children to spell the word on index cards. She then put them all up on the chalkboard ledge so they could look at the different ways people went about spelling it. Then she asked them, "What are you noticing?" and then "Any other patterns or things that surprise you?" She was asking children to examine the logic of words and their spelling strategies, but the assignment to choose an interesting word for the day in the first place had children looking for interesting words, noticing novelty. This alone will expand their range of language. She might have asked them, as another teacher did, to notice also any unusual uses of words.

Notice how these comments assume something about "you"—that you are (obviously, so I don't need to say it explicitly—nor can you contest it) a noticing kind of person. You are (equally obviously) the kind of person who wishes to write interesting things. These are quite loaded invitations to construct particular identities, which we will return to in the next chapter.

Children becoming literate need to learn the significant features of text, how it's organized (letters, words, arguments, structure, punctuation, etc.), how it relates to spoken language, how to recognize the little tricks authors use to compel readers, when to use which sort of written language, and so forth. However, no learner can afford to be dependent on the teacher for everything that needs to be noticed, so teachers have to teach children to look for possibilities. We draw children's attention to different patterns in texts, words, and sounds, how print is different from illustrations, how it is laid out on the page, and so forth. We will also teach them ways of using these patterns when they notice them, but first they have to notice them. We will not be able to show them every pattern or feature, and even if we could, we might not want to because we want them to become adept at noticing them for themselves.

When children in class can't help themselves from noticing and pointing out patterns, teaching becomes a whole lot easier. The teacher no longer is the sole source of knowledge. For example, a second grader in Ellen Adams' class observed, "Did you ever notice that lots of books have wolves in them?"[15] A first grader in Chris Murphy's class noticed Chris's use of "chitty-chatty" as she drew their attention to the noise level. He pointed out the phonetic similarity of the words and noticed the smaller units of chit-chat. These examples indicate that, in classes like these, children learn that their noticing matters. It's a valued topic of conversation. When they notice something, it's worth bringing up for discussion (even at odd times).

Starting with the child's observations rather than the teacher's has many advantages. In studies of infants, it's called "attentional following" and infants whose mothers do it develop stronger vocabularies than infants whose mothers constantly try to get their child to attend to something the mother deems important—requiring "attentional switching" on the part of the infant.[16] When children notice things, instruction can begin with a joint focus of attention because the children are already attending. I once watched Joan Backer do an excellent lesson on handwriting without actually doing a lesson. She explained to her fourth graders that she was having a problem reading some of their handwriting. With a chart of the alphabet in cursive, she invited them to help her plan some instruction to improve their writing, asking them what to start with. She took notes on chart paper as the students brainstormed the problem. In the process, they discussed which were the difficult letters (and what made them difficult), which letters were easily confused (and what made for the confusion), and, for instructional efficiency, which were the most frequent letters (disagreement required a committee to investigate further), and which groups of letters had a lot in common and therefore would get the most instructional mileage. In the process, the children were socializing each other's attention to features of handwriting, and Joan merely cleaned up the details. Classifying the letters also required naming them in terms of their salient characteristics.

Joan's "noticing" question has a second important part—"Any other patterns or things that surprise you?" The frequent use of "any other" serves to keep students looking for multiple possibilities, building flexibility (to which we will return later). But the "surprise" part is also important. We want children to attend to their mind's feeling of surprise, which is a good indicator of conflicting patterns or theories. Such conflicts offer great locations for conceptual learning because they require us to rethink things that we take for granted.[17] Feelings of discomfort or uneasiness can be useful indicators too. Often, we smother these feelings rather than deal with their source such as when we witness a social wrong.

Marie Clay points out that attending to these feelings is also about building internal control and a self-extending system. When a child runs into trouble in his reading and the teacher says, "What's wrong? ... Something didn't make sense, did it? ... What can you do?" The teacher is helping the child notice those internal signals and contemplate how to respond to them, a system that will continue to operate when the teacher is not there. Helping children use their intuitions to learn more about themselves and the world might also help with another phenomenon. According to Winston Churchill "men occasionally stumble over the truth, but most of them pick themselves up and hurry off as if nothing had happened."[18] Attending to these bodily feelings of surprise and unease might help us reduce this problem.

Noticing and naming has important implications for critical literacy. Ultimately, children must notice how naming is done, who is named in which ways, and who gets to do the naming. When we had teenagers, I recall a conversation arising at our dinner table about the word "skank" in which we discussed what this name means, who uses it, why, what the male equivalent might be and whether it has the same connotations. We might call this noticing our naming. We also have to help children, and ourselves, understand how names (as categories) come to be associated with particular definitions. For example, I asked one child, "Are there different kinds of readers in this class?" He responded, "There's ones like the people who's not good and the people who are good..."[19] His response should give us pause when we offer praise like, "That's what good readers do." While it reinforces the strategy the child used, it validates the use of a good–bad binary as a sensible descriptor for readers. It opens the question of who the bad readers are and how you can tell.

A good–bad continuum is not the most productive way to name readers and writers. In fact, I asked one fourth grader, Chloe, to identify the good writers in class so that I could then ask her about her criteria for distinguishing good writers. Her response was simply, "I don't like to think of it that way." This is tantamount to saying, "that's not a good question and I won't be part of the discussion it leads to. It's not normal to talk about writers that way." It's the moral equivalent of telling someone of higher social status that they just told a sexist joke. Chloe's confident rebuke is possible because of her classroom community. Chloe, along with children from similar classrooms, felt that readers and writers come in categories of interest, style, and genre. I know this will be a bit controversial, but perhaps it's better if we say simply, "that's what readers do." It's a stance that allows us to recognize that readers also do things like make mistakes, such as when first-grade teacher Pegeen Jensen during a read-aloud said, "I just made a big mistake as a reader. I got distracted when someone came into the room. So, I'm going to reread this section here."[20] Pegeen's stance normalizes mistakes (and recovery strategies) as an expected part of what readers do and that doesn't imply a reader's goodness or badness.

Through our noticing and naming language, children learn the significant features of the world, themselves, and others. These understandings influence how they treat each other and their environment. For the sake of a just society, I am particularly concerned about children's naming of themselves and others and their awareness of the sources and consequences of those namings. Among other things, those namings affect children's identities.

Selective Noticing and Naming

Teachers interact differently with children because of their race and gender—well, obviously, not you dear reader, but *other* teachers, the ones who've been studied (and, alas, myself).[21] Doctors do the same with their patients.[22] Even chatbots assume doctors are male and nurses female. Why should teachers be any different? The bias shows up in who gets chosen to speak, whose responses are taken up or ignored, who gets praised or reprimanded for what and how seriously. We should be concerned about these biases, but we should not be surprised by them. Bias is built into us from the get-go. Even three-month-old babies show a preference for faces of their own race.[23]

Biases—systematic asymmetries—are hidden in the language that envelopes and occupies us. Words themselves can have a positive or negative valence, like "happy" or "menacing," or they can be neutral, like the verb "cause." But word meanings are also affected by the words they hang out with, and the ten most frequently co-occurring with "cause" are: Death, problems, damage, pain, cancer, trouble, concern, disease, effect, and harm. Consequently, although people consciously rate "cause" as neutral, in measures of implicit bias, they respond to it as negative. Language doesn't have to be obviously biased to create implicit bias.

Why does this matter? It helps explain why even six-year-old children show implicit race and gender bias.[24] Because, in large language samples, female-related words occur in the same context as words related to family, nursing, and words like emotional, rather than with words related to doctor, science, math, or words like honorable.[25] For male-related words it's the reverse. It also helps explain why minority group members manage to acquire an implicit bias against their own group even as children. African American names are more often found in the context of negative words whereas European names collocate more with positive words.

These biases show up in television shows, children's books, and talk directed at children.[26] Beyond reflecting cultural biases, these patterns also enforce them through associative learning.[27] That's why it's particularly hard to change personal biases because they originate in the cultural discourse and are maintained by it, and to the casual observer, they're invisible. But we can, and must, consciously change that linguistic balance in our own classrooms. It's one reason we ensure the books available to our students, and that we read with them, reflect a diversity of protagonists. It's also why when we are studying history and social studies, we make sure that children hear the full humanity of history—the good, the bad, and the ugly.

We have to notice our own language and the language around us, holding ourselves and our students accountable for our language, while offering tools for change and opportunities to repair damage. Much of the opportunity for conversations about restructuring our language will come from thinking together around narrative texts that include matters of race and gender. But newspaper reports that include or report on racist language are also excellent opportunities. For example, in 2020 Alabama voters (76.5 percent of them) authorized their legislature to remove racist language from the state's constitution, in order to, as a state Representative observed, "Show, not only the rest of the country, but the world who we are today."[28] Examples like this show bipartisan efforts to move institutional language toward a more equitable society while showing how we make advances, and providing a sense of where we're coming from.

Classroom discourse is not only the spoken language. It also has to do with other choices we make. For example, do we differentially call on students from different racial, ethnic, linguistic, or gender groups to offer their ideas? Our differential treatment is related to our attitudes and beliefs. For example, consider how we talk about and interact with the language of students who are, or are becoming, multilingual. We tend to view those students through the language they aren't yet fluent with, English, rather than viewing them through what they can do in the language(s) they already know. We need to recognize that they bring a wealth of knowledge from their home communities and, unlike many others in their classes, they have often traveled internationally. Keeping the curriculum open to their experience goes a long way toward improving their school learning experience, their self-competence, and the attitudes of their classmates.

Extension

To explore this idea of noticing and naming, I recommend books like Katie Wood Ray's *In Pictures and in Words* in which they name the details of the author's craft. For example, apply what we discussed in this chapter to the following section from *Wondrous Words* in which a student, Ian, is stuck. In the process of helping him imagine a place to go as a writer, Katie Wood Ray offers to help. They look at his notebook and she says:

Katie: Ian, this statement you wrote here, this statement says to me that you have a vignette or a snapshot thing in mind. It sounds like there must be a lot of little scenes in your head about those special times with Jazz [his dog]. Am I right?

Ian: Yes.

Katie: I think you could probably play with that structure some and see what happens. You know, a piece about you and Jazz, sort of like Cynthia Rylant's that we looked at, *When I Was Young in the Mountains*. Remember how we talked about how it was written with all those little snapshot stories? (p. 259)

She imagines some vignettes as possibilities that jog Ian's memories. She adds:

Katie: OK, great! You'll need some way of tying them all together eventually, maybe a repeating line like Rylant uses. (p. 260)

She then opens some ideas that get Ian's interest as places to start, and leaves him with a plan:

Katie: I'd do two things, then, first. I'd reread *When I Was Young in the Mountains* to see again how Rylant did this kind of text. Then I'd start a list in your notebook of ideas for little scenes you might write of you and Jazz. OK? (p. 260)

3 Identity

At the same time that the children were using the stories to proclaim their identity as boys and "tough kids," those stories were also, in a sense, claiming them. That is, the boys were adopting dominant cultural storylines about how tough kids talk.[1]

Anne Haas Dyson

Discussing different authors in his class, Steven observes, "For the funny part, Jessie is really funny. He writes a lot about fantasy stuff... Ron's a pretty good writer... and he's a little better at drawing than writing... [and] Emily [in her mystery] gave details. She described the characters. It was a really good mystery because it had a point and it had something that the reader had to figure out."[2] In the course of his comments, Steven identifies himself and his peers as authors in the same terms as he talks about the authors of the commercial books they read. His teacher orchestrates classroom conversations in which he will develop his understanding of what authors do and further consolidate and elaborate his identity as an author. At the same time, because he sees his peers as a diverse group of authors, and treats them as such, he further consolidates their identities as competent and varied authors.

Children in our classrooms are *becoming* literate. They are not simply learning the skills of literacy. They're developing personal and social identities—uniquenesses and affiliations that define the people they see themselves becoming. They're all affiliated in that they're all authors, but all different in their uniquenesses. James Gee calls such classrooms "affinity spaces," the same sort of communities that make video games "cognitively and emotionally compelling" to children.[3] Because they can all be different, there is space for each of them to be competent members of the community, contributing their distinctiveness to the classroom fabric to which they belong. This would not be possible if the classroom had a singular focus, for example on word reading and spelling accuracy.

Notice that Steven describes the other students through their different contributions. He attends closely and admires what they are doing. Notice, too, they are making books—what Katie Wood Ray and Lisa Cleaveland call "Big work."[4] Katie asked two first graders in Lisa's class what they were working on. Their answer: "We're writing a series. It's sort of like *Frog and Toad* and *Henry and Mudge*, but it's about us." The authors, Maggie and Larke, showed her the first two books and the third they were working on. They need strong identities to sustain them through the travails of doing big work over many days and then taking up new big work.

When authors write novels, they create characters—people who say this sort of thing, do that sort of thing, and relate to people and things in these sorts of ways. As we come to understand the richness and complexity of a character in a novel, we come to expect how they will likely behave when facing a new situation (though new situations can bring surprises). This is not just what authors do, it's what people do with themselves.[5] They narrate their lives, identifying themselves and the circumstances, acting and explaining events in ways they see as consistent with the person they take themselves to be.

Identities even focus attention. Lisa Cleaveland offers an example from her first-grade class.[6] Helena is the only one left in the snack area. She comments to Lisa "Mrs. Cleaveland, I'm all alone," which she follows immediately with "Hey, that would be a good repeating line for a book." It's nowhere near writing workshop time, and yet, ever the author, Helena is constantly on the hunt for useful language—something she knows authors like her do.

Building our identities means coming to see in ourselves the characteristics of particular categories (and roles) of people and developing a sense of what it feels like to be that sort of person and to belong in certain social spaces. As children are involved in classroom interactions, they build and try on different identities—different protagonist positions. We hear something of this when they use the pronoun "I" in the storylines in which they plot themselves. They decide who they are in a given context. They decide between agentive characters who are active and assume responsibility, and more passive characters who do not. And they take up positions with respect to what they are studying, with respect to others in their social environment, and with respect to domains of practice.

Teachers' language can offer children, and nudge them toward, productive identities. For example, during a read-aloud, eighth grader Deandra asked about a relationship between two characters in the book and how it was similar to a relationship in another book she had read.[7] Her question led to a discussion that her teacher wrapped up with: "I love how Deandra made us think about the word for that—confidante." Later, Deandra commented that, "It makes me think more educated in my mind when I read because of how Ms. Tucker talks to me." These small moments help establish Deandra's identity as a legitimate, competent contributor to the learning community (while at the same time expanding everyone's vocabulary). Even the small matter of pronouncing a child's name as they prefer it pronounced is an important mark of respect that helps the child feel seen and heard.

It might already have occurred to you that children bring with them to school well-learned cultural narratives acquired in cooperatively retelling family stories from a very young age. These narratives hold models of the possible forms narratives can take, who is allowed to take which roles, and so forth.[8] Children have already learned some of the roles open and not open to girls, for example, the feelings and actions that go along with those roles, and how certain behaviors should be understood, such as a boy who reads or a girl who argues, or a boy who plays with dolls. They have learned these aspects of identity in subtle ways. Parents tend to retell events differently with daughters and sons, particularly when it comes to emotional events. An event reconstructed as invoking sadness for a daughter, such as having a toy stolen, is likely to be reconstructed to include anger for a son—emotions with very different relationships to agency.[9] Boys and girls differ too, on average, in the stories they tend to tell about success and failure.[10] Our job is to help children of whatever gender, race, and identity to construct productive and equitable narratives about the possibilities and implications of their choices.

❧ *"We're all teachers here."*
At the beginning of the year, Laurie McCarthy invites her first- and second-grade students to see themselves as teachers. Then she helps

them confirm it. She notices students using strategies for working together or problem-solving, which they do automatically (without awareness) when they are engaged. She explains to them the strategy she saw them use and why it's important. This brings it to the children's consciousness, builds their sense of agency, and makes available the language they will need to explain it. Then she invites them to teach the class about the strategy which, with her support, they do. It only takes a minute or two and it confers an enormous sense of competence while distributing the knowledge and establishing classmates as bona fide sources of information to be accessed as necessary.

When Laurie notices a child helping another learn something, she brings it to the class's attention. She explains how it helps the community, and the important part of teaching it illustrates. For example, having described the helping, she might say, "When Tatiana helped Jerome, he was able to carry on reading immediately instead of having to wait for me to finish working with a group. Thanks Tatiana. Also, I noticed that she didn't just tell him the word, she helped him to figure it out himself. Why do you think that's important?" Laurie shows that she values helping, while increasing students' knowledge of teaching and the likelihood that future student-to-student teaching will pay off. Her efforts also have long-term benefits. Many of her students will become parents and teachers in adulthood.

Nudging children to identify as teachers distributes authority and expertise in the classroom. Distributed teaching is also a characteristic of Gee's video game affinity spaces. When the teacher is the only one in the room with the knowledge, there is a bottleneck. We will see a line of children to the teacher's desk, waiting for approval, correction, or problem-solving. This is not just wasted time. It limits student independence and agency.

❦ *"As scientists, how should we handle this?"*

To answer the question, children, at least temporarily, have to imagine themselves into that identity and might choose to maintain the possibility of wearing that mantle. Notice, again, how the assertion that the students are scientists ("as scientists") is provided as given (already agreed upon) rather than new information, making it less open to contestation.

Just the identity label will not accomplish all that is needed, of course. We need to construct an understanding of what scientists

Identity

(or mathematicians or authors) do, how they talk and act. In one classroom, the teachers referred to themselves as "senior researchers," and children sometimes as "researcher Tom," and began lessons reiterating that "we are researchers, let us do research."[11] When children argued that the teacher's role is to tell children the answers, the response was that, "It is a characteristic of researchers that they attempt to answer the questions themselves."[12] The response encourages the collective identity of a community of practice, that "people like us" do things this way. It also denies the frame presented by the children that "we are traditional students and you are a traditional teacher and we are doing school." It replies, in effect, "I'm sorry but you must be in the wrong theater. I don't know those actors or that plot. Here's how this script goes." It asserts, "When I say *we* from now on in these conversations, this is the sort of people I am referring to."

Identities such as researcher-in-a-research-community are an important accomplishment of schooling, but also a tool for shaping children's classroom participation. These identities provide students with a sense of their responsibilities, and reasonable ways to act, particularly toward one another and toward the object of study. Implicit in these identities are notions of community since identity is tied to both uniqueness and affiliation.[13] In such classrooms, then, teachers are not merely trying to teach subject matter. Rather, they are, as Ed Elbers and Leen Streefland put it in math, "mathematizing: turning everyday issues into mathematical problems and using mathematics evolving from these activities for solving realistic problems."[14] Learning science, writing, mathematics, and so forth in this manner breaks the division between school and "the real world," a division that limits the significance and impact of children's learning.

❦ *"What are you doing as a writer today?"*

This query has several features. First, it frames what the student will be doing in terms of what writers do, and invites a conversation on those terms rather than in terms of, say, a student doing a task for the teacher. Second, again, by presenting as "given" the assertions that a) the student is a writer, who b) will be doing something that writers do, it makes it hard to reject either the identity or the action. They are not up for discussion. The student has to say something like "[As a writer] I'm researching tigers for the book I'm making."

27

The conversation opener insists on a commitment to a particular character (I, a writer) engaged in a particular kind of narrative (doing writerly things). The student is gently nudged—well, all right, pushed—to rehearse a narrative with herself as the writer/protagonist, opening the possibility of the teacher elaborating the story with details and plot suggestions.

❦ *"I wonder if, as a writer, you're ready for this…"*

This at once asks the child to think about learning in terms of development or maturity, and invites a desire to be viewed as having an expanded maturity. It leans quite heavily on the student to both view herself as an author, and to pick up the gauntlet of challenge. If she does pick up the gauntlet and overcome the challenge, in the context of the teacher's words it will be hard for her to avoid composing a narrative about self-as-author-overcoming-challenge. Overcoming obstacles in this way provides a seductive invitation to adopt the identity. If the teacher asks her how she did it, she will rearticulate the story—with herself as the successful protagonist.

❦ *"I bet you're proud of yourself."*

It feels good to be proud of accomplishing something. Feelings of pride can build an internal motivation going forward.[15] But pride is a tricky emotion to draw attention to because it comes in two forms: Authentic and hubristic.[16] *Hubristic* pride is the chest-thumping pride we often see in athletic encounters. It has a down side. It's generally associated with aggressiveness, hostility, and social anxiety. People with a sense of hubristic pride tend to be more interested in putting others down, gaining a sense of superiority, and dominating others than offering them support.[17] The feeling of *authentic* pride is associated with being creative and having a community-oriented, agreeable, prosocial stance, and good self-esteem. Not surprisingly, it's often accompanied by a degree of popularity. So, if we're going to draw attention to pride, we have to ensure it's the right kind of pride—pride in strategically overcoming obstacles to accomplish something challenging, pride in community-oriented prosocial behaviors, or in collaborative problem-solving.

We avoid comments or situations that set up a sense of hubristic pride, ones that invite pride through interpersonal comparisons and a zero-sum sense of self-worth, or merely through the achievement itself regardless of the struggle. Instead, we focus the pride invitation on the *process* of accomplishing something positive. So, if we are to invoke pride, we might add, "I bet you're proud of yourself [for not giving up on that project] or [for helping your partner solve that problem]." The idea is to build a narrative about triumph over a problem, adversity, or one's own limitations, rather than triumph over other people. The general "I bet you're proud of yourself for [valued process, strategy, struggle...]," asserts independence and an agentive narrative. At the same time, it doesn't detract from the feeling that the teacher is also empathically proud *with* the child.

We want children to attend to the process and the agency it offers, and we want children to build positive identities, recognizing their agency in that construction. When we're discussing books, news, or other events, we might say, "That's the kind of person I want to be" or "I hope in that situation, I would choose to be the kind of person who would..." We want children to have Deandra's experience of feeling "more educated in my mind" as she builds her identity and life narrative.

Books That Changed Me

Second- and third-grade teacher Merry Komar created an anchor chart in her room titled "Books that changed me." The children recorded on the chart books that they felt had changed who they were as a person and how it had changed them. This is not a chart of "my favorite books." Rather, there is an expectation that books can be a tool for changing who we are. The assumption is that we have some agency over our own becoming, that our selves are to an extent self-authoring. Ellen, who had been in the class a year earlier, was asked whether she could recall any of the books that year that had changed her as a person. She responded:

> *The Pain and the Great One* has changed me because when you have siblings, you feel the other person gets more attention. Jake [younger brother with autism] and I feel the same way. So now when I'm angry with him, I don't yell at Jake for doing the things that he doesn't necessarily need to be yelled at for. Instead, in my head I know he's feeling this way so why would I do anything to make it harder on him.

This recognition that books can be a tool for self-construction, a sense that students have agency in their own self-narrative is very powerful. Eighth grader Elise, in Ms. Tucker's class which had a similar ethos, explained:

> I've read books about mean people, and I used to be, I was a person who was, like, very guarded, and if you didn't like me, then that's your problem. And I'm who I am, so if you have a problem with me, get over it. And then, like, reading about all those mean girls who think like that, the things that happen to them, it made me sit back and question it. So, it's been, like, I've been a nicer person. But I'm more energetic.

As we shall see in Chapter 5, this sense of self as growing and changing is an anchor for a powerful meaning-making system.

Community Identity

We are a social species, and our identities are collective as well as individual. Our individual identities and behaviors are influenced by the collective identity. As teachers, we want to build a collective classroom ethos that is academic, but also kind and caring. So we tell narratives about who we are as a group.

Rather than using classroom examples here, I'll step out onto the political stage because the principle is the same. I'm originally from New Zealand, and during the recent Covid-19 pandemic, New Zealand was particularly successful at limiting loss of life. The prime minister at the time was Jacinda Ardern. Her language in getting the people to participate in difficult preventive measures including lockdowns, and in surviving other national tragedies, has been analyzed because of its effectiveness. A good deal of her language drew on and built a collective identity linked to individual behavior, exactly as a classroom teacher might. She said things like the following:[18]

- [New Zealand] is a place that is diverse, that is welcoming, that is kind and compassionate.
- We are a tough, resilient people… our journey will depend on how we work together.

- I'm asking you to do everything you can to protect all of us. None of us can do this alone. Your actions will be critical to our collective effort to stop Covid-19.
- We are a team of five million.
- I have one final message: Be kind. I know people will want to act as enforcers. I understand that. People are afraid and anxious... what we need from you, our community, is for you to support others. Go home tonight and check in on your neighbors. Start a phone tree with your street. Plan how you'll keep in touch with one another. We will get through this together, but only if we stick together. So please be strong and be kind.

People need a sense of belonging, and Ardern's comments build a narrative about the caring community to which they belong—what sort of characters New Zealanders are collectively. She points to the importance of individual acts for the collective welfare, and the expected ethos of the community. She recognizes, and normalizes, people's negative feelings in dealing with adversity, and offers them constructive ways to build and sustain a community consistent with the caring identity. In classrooms, we do the same. We reinforce a caring classroom identity by thinking together about books like *Each Kindness*, *The Invisible Boy*, *Peace Week in Miss Fox's Class*, *The Story of Ruby Bridges*, and others that open conversations about kindness, being a caring community, and dealing with things that divide people. We choose books with relatable characters and personally relevant moral dilemmas. Along the way, we use language just like Ardern's to build a sense of positive collective agency. We also help children to see how their own language choices play a role in the qualities of the community.

Identity and Stereotype

When we name groups of people, we often attribute to them a general set of attributes—stereotypes which we then apply to group members. Stereotypes affect our perceptions of students' behavior, their abilities, their personalities, and their motivation to learn. These influence our academic expectations and our responses to student behavior.[19]

When a stereotype is invoked it can become a self-fulfilling prophecy. Students can unconsciously live into it. Just prompting

African American college students to attend to their racial iden-tity with a demographic question at the top of a test can produce lower test scores because they feel themselves at risk of conforming to stereotype.[20] Gender and racial stereotypes influence even very young children's academic performance. For example, Nalini Am-bady and her colleagues subtly activated stereotypes in K-2 Asian-American girls by getting them to color in pictures before taking a math test.[21] For some the picture was two Asian children eating with chopsticks, for some it was of a girl holding a doll. A control group colored a gender- and race-neutral picture. On the math test, the girls prompted to attend to their Asian-ness did better than the control group, and the girls prompted to attend to their gender did worse. Using language to nudge stereotypes, the researchers found the same thing with middle school students. Stereotypes also result in people having to live with the threat of being viewed as a rep-resentative of the stereotype, and anxiety about accidentally doing something that confirms it. This is also one reason why we don't put an individual student in the position of being a spokesperson for their entire race or ethnic group, or responsible for what mem-bers of their race or ethnic group did back in history.

Stereotypes are invoked by small unconscious acts of language: Gender markers like "Boys and girls, it's time for math." We don't actually need to use these markers. There are lots of options, like "Mathematicians, let's do some math." Studies that attempt to change people's racial biases also offer guidance. For example, training includes telling illustrative stories, and efforts are more suc-cessful when training participants strongly identify with the people portrayed in the stories. They are also more successful if the train-ing doesn't just, for example, link Black people with positives, but also links white people with flaws, making it clear that people make mistakes, do good things, and sometimes not so good. It's called being human.[22]

These findings have implications for the kinds of books we share with students and how we share them. For example, we choose books that portray the perspectives of diverse characters in diverse roles, and we encourage children to take up those perspectives and explore characters' thoughts and feelings, as we shall see in Chapter 6. Research on ingroups and outgroups similarly shows that taking the perspective of an outgroup member improves attitudes toward the outgroup.[23] Not only that, it also reduces prejudice and discriminatory conduct toward other outgroup members. But these benefits don't generalize to other outgroups which is, again, why we need books with a diversity of characters in a diversity of roles—including authors and illustrators so that it's easier for all children to find themselves in those roles. According to Ellen Langer, stereotypes are the result of looking at differences but stopping too quickly. The foundation for undermining stereotypes is reminding ourselves that everyone is unique. We are different from our siblings, parents, and closest friends.

Evolving Language (and Society)

In an evolved society, we want to avoid language that demeans or hurts others. But we've been born into a language replete with expressions that do just that to different groups—"that's dumb/lame," or "I've been gypped" (from gypsy with a stereotype of being cheated). We can stop using these. Some of our language casts people with disabilities in a poor light. In much the same way as we take the trouble to pronounce a child's name correctly, we try to talk about and with people with disabilities in ways that give them the respect they deserve. Just talking about "normal people" in relation to people with disabilities casts the latter as abnormal. Better to refer to non-disabled people. After all, we're all only temporarily able, a fact that becomes increasingly clear to me as I age. And as we age and acquire disabilities, I doubt that we would generally want our disabilities to become the central feature of our identity. The same is true of those who already have disabilities, so when a person with a disability is the focus of a conversation, we don't need to refer to the disability unless it's pertinent to the story we are telling. We don't want to diminish their agency either, so we can avoid terms like "victim of," "stricken with," or "wheelchair bound," words that invoke pity. Instead, we can use terms like "living with" [a wheelchair, cerebral palsy] and "wheelchair user." There are not always simple substitutions, and language is always in transition. We've tried language like "differently abled" and "challenged" but these euphemisms are often seen as condescending ways of avoiding talking about important things like access and accommodations, and disability itself, an avoidance that can invoke shame.

The various communities of persons with disabilities do not all agree on appropriate language. For example, some prefer "persons with disabilities" others "disabled persons," and individuals within those groups have their own sensibilities. Although, in general, people with handicaps don't want the handicap to be the center of their identity, there are groups for whom this is not the case. For example, the Deaf is written with an uppercase D because it denotes a community with its own culture and language, and thus a core part of community members' identities. These complexities should not cause us to throw up our hands and give up. We're all still learning. But if we're unsure, we can always ask for their preference, and if we err, we can always apologize. Fortunately, there are plenty of accessible resources to help us build inclusive, respectful language.[24]

Changing our language is a slow and uncomfortable process because we have to consciously reprogram otherwise automatic responses. We'll trip over our words. Part of the difficulty is that there's an emotional element. A few years ago, I was at a gathering at a brand-new university education building. It had gender-neutral bathrooms on the first floor. That is, you go into the bathroom and there are mirrors and hand basins on one side and stalls on the other side. It's a change I'm completely in favor of—in theory. But each time I used those bathrooms, with women touching up makeup and such, I felt uneasy. I wasn't the only one. I met a friend walking upstairs to the gendered bathrooms. Though also comfortable with the shift to neutral bathrooms in theory, she said, "I'm just not ready for the gender-neutral ones." Our discomfort comes from the violation of a deeply embodied history of practice. It's the same sort of discomfort many people have in referring to a single person as "they." It's an emotional response to a small change that goes against a history of automatic, taken-for-granted experience.

Trying to avoid these experiences of discomfort leads us to do things like make less eye contact with students from different races or ethnicities. When those of us in the dominant culture have these occasional experiences of discomfort, it's worth remembering that people from marginalized groups routinely have such experiences. Children experience that sense of dis-ease when there are cultural violations in classroom practice. And there will be. In the US in 2023, teachers are middle class, 80 percent white, and 75 percent female.[25] Only 45 percent of students are white. Black, Brown, and multilingual children, and those with disabilities, do not have the same classroom experiences as their white middle- and upper-class peers.

Learning relationships require "an atmosphere of approval" and trust, and the cultural differences inherent in these demographics, unaddressed, can disrupt those relationships.[26] For example, white middle-class teachers often use indirect commands like "Would you like to open your books now?" and can be puzzled, even cranky, when children used to more direct language respond as if the command were simply a question. Recognizing such interactional confusions as ones of miscommunication rather than as willful disobedience will prevent problematic interactions. Failure to recognize students' speech and interaction patterns, and "funds of knowledge," or worse, viewing them as inferior, as often happens, will undermine learning relationships.[27] These are, after all, elements of children's identities. We have to be aware of the local linguistic and knowledge resources children bring to the classroom and find ways to capitalize on them.

There are resources to help.[28]

Extension

There are two ways to explore your own teaching in terms of children's developing literate identities. The first is to audio record some class conversations around books and around writing, such as writing conferences, and to listen to them in terms of the issues I have raised in this chapter. Video-recording is also useful, and provides additional information about posture, participation, facial expression, and so forth, but it can be too much information to process in one go. A second, perhaps more direct, way is to have conversations with a couple of students in your class around questions like, "Are there different kinds of reader (writer) in this class do you think?"

To get you started on this project, and in case you do not currently have your own classroom, I offer the following abstract of a conversation with Mandy. As you read it, ask:

• What noticing and naming is taking place?
• What identity is this student developing?
• What classroom conversations made this identity possible?

As you make your decisions, point to the evidence you are drawing on. Then plan some ways of engaging this student that would alter her understanding of literacy and of herself as a literate person.

Mandy

Mandy says that a good writer "writes fast... [for example] when the teacher tells us to write a story then it doesn't even take her... not even ten minutes." Mandy does not talk with other students about their writing. She "wouldn't want to hurt their feelings or nothing because sometimes when someone comes up to them and says 'Oh, you're a bad writer,' and everything. Then, they'll tell the teacher..." Mandy says that they should not give other students ideas, "because then that would be giving them things that you thought of in your head... Then they'll have, probably, the same stories."

Good readers, she says, are "all the kids that are quiet and they just listen... they challenge themselves... they get chapter books." Asked to describe herself as a reader or a writer, she says she doesn't understand the question. She does not know how she could learn about another child as a reader or writer.

Asked whether they do research in her class, she says she is unsure what it is. When it's explained she says they don't do it. Mandy expects on her report card an "excellent" for writing and a comment like, "Mandy has behaved and she is nice to other classmates." To help a classmate become a better reader, she would tell them to "stop fooling around because the more you fool around the more you get your name on the board and checks... [and] if he doesn't know that word, if he doesn't know how to sound it out or if he doesn't know what it means, look it up in the dictionary."

In talking about books, Mandy makes no connections across books or with personal experience.

Agency and Becoming Strategic

I'm so proud of myself. I didn't believe that I could do it, and I did it. And I'm just going to go spread joy because all my other scores, I've never passed a [state] test in my whole entire past life, and I finally passed one... Yeah. I'm gonna bring myself out more. Now that I've done that, I believe I can do anything.

Eighth grader Darla

I've been able to look at myself and say, "Okay, this is what's gotta be done. Okay, we need to relax and take time and smell the roses, but we also need to plan for the future."

Eighth grader Marta

A child must have some version of, "Yes, I imagine I can do this." And a teacher must also view the present child as competent and on that basis imagine new possibilities.

Anne Haas Dyson[1]

If nothing else, children should leave school with a sense that if they act, and act strategically, they can accomplish their goals—a sense of agency.[2] Some teachers are very good at building a sense of agency in children, and in this chapter I describe how their language helps. The spark of agency is simply the perception that the environment is responsive to our actions. Many researchers argue that this spark is a fundamental human desire.[3] They base this on the fact that even young babies notice and express excitement when their behavior appears to have an effect. They get excited if the mobile above their crib moves when they wriggle. Parents and caregivers foster this development when they are responsive to their baby's actions. And caregiver responsiveness influences infants' language development.[4] And it's reciprocal. Infants' communicative efforts influence the responsiveness of caregivers.[5] This desire for agency persists throughout life, and it's so powerful that when people feel there is no relationship between what they do and what happens, they become depressed and helpless.[6] Parents with depression are generally less responsive to their babies, with adverse consequences for babies' development.[7]

Having a sense of agency, then, is fundamental. Our well-being depends on it. But building this sense doesn't depend simply on a coincidence between our actions and an event, as it does for babies. For much of what we do, there is a delay between our action—writing a good lead—and its consequences—drawing people into our writing. Not only is there a delay, but often the consequence is not immediately obvious. People like what we have written, but we have to figure out why—it could have been just a lucky break. This is where the mediation of teachers' language becomes crucial, and where human beings' propensity for storytelling fits in. Teachers' conversations with children help the children build the narrative bridges between action and consequence. They show children how, by acting strategically, they accomplish things, and that they are the kind of person who does accomplish things.

As human beings, we constantly tell stories about ourselves to others and to ourselves, and the stories shape who we think we are. In a sense, we experience ourselves in narrative form, or, as Catherine Riessman puts it, "individuals become the autobiographical narratives by which they tell about their lives."[8] In order to solve the many problems I will encounter as a writer, and to persist through the many revisions I will face (trust me on this), I have to weave myself into a narrative in which I am the kind of person who actively encounters and solves problems with text. I develop this belief, in part, through a history of conversations with others, and myself, around my writing.

To understand children's development of a sense of agency, then, we need to look at the kinds of stories we arrange for children to tell themselves. Just as we can plot ourselves in stories in which we are the active protagonists, the ones with agency, we can plot ourselves in the same story attributing the agency to another factor—my test score was good because the teacher asked easy questions, or I was just lucky. Telling stories in which we relegate ourselves to a passive role is the inverse of agency. Jerome Bruner calls it "victimicity."[9]

The problem for us to solve, then, is how do we arrange for children to tell many literacy stories in which they are the successful agentive protagonists? The heart of a good narrative is a character who encounters a problem and by acting strategically solves the problem, usually (but not necessarily) attaining a goal. The following examples of teacher comments likely influenced the agency children experience in the stories they tell about themselves as literate individuals.

❦ *"How did you figure that out?"*

Asking children this question when they have successfully solved a problem invites them to review the process, or strategies, used to accomplish a goal or solve a problem. The question insists that a child respond with something like, "First I…" In other words, it nudges students to tell a story with themselves as agentive protagonists. Aside from the strategy review this provides, it invites a sense of agency as part of the child's literate identity.

This "how did you" invitation to an agentive role is particularly important. We often encounter classrooms in which children are being taught strategies, but they are not being strategic. Knowing strategies guarantees neither their active, flexible deployment nor a sense of agency. Marie Clay raised this problem when she wrote about teaching *for* strategies rather than just teaching strategies.[10] Teaching for strategies requires setting children up to generate strategies, then reviewing with them, in an agentive retelling, the effectiveness of the strategies they generated—"You figured out that tricky word by yourself. How did you do that?" As children do this, they're in control of the problem-solving process and they are asked to consciously recognize that control in an agentive narrative. In the process, they become more able to generalize the strategy.[11]

This strategy of arranging for a student to figure something out independently, without full awareness and then reflecting on it, has been called *revealing*. Courtney Cazden contrasts this with *telling*, in which the teacher is explicit up front and then the students practice what they have been taught to do.[12] I suspect that revealing is more difficult than telling because it requires taking into account the child's current understanding. Its benefit is that the child actually does the constructing or problem-solving, making possible the sense of agency. Telling, on the other hand, produces awareness, which is not always immediately useful. As Marie Clay pointed out, "most things we do as readers need to operate below the conscious level most of the time so that fast and effective processing of the print is achieved and attention is paid to the messages rather than to the work done to get to the message."[13]

The side benefit of the "How did you…?" question is that as children articulate their strategic action, they teach their strategies to other students without the teacher being the source-from-which-all-knowledge-comes. Naturalizing this sort of conversation opens the possibility that students will continue those conversations among themselves, thus increasing the level of available "explicit" instruction without increasing the extent to which children are being told what to do.

"Sounds good," you might say, "so how do we increase the opportunities to have this sort of conversation?" That's where the next question comes in. In order to set up agentive narratives, children have to face problems.

❦ *"What problems did you come across today?"*

When asked as a predictable question this implies that it's normal to encounter problems. Everybody does. This, in turn, makes it normal to talk about confronting and solving those problems. It also helps students identify problems and view them as places to learn, and it sets up the possibility of asking, "How did/could you solve that problem?" the invitation to construct an agentive narrative. We can also expand the conversation to, "Has anyone else had that problem? How did you solve it?" and "How else could we solve it?" and "This is what I do when I have that problem," each of which proliferates further the agentive possibilities. It's possible for children to answer that they asked someone else how to solve the problem. This, too, can be retold asserting agency: "Asking someone is a good way to solve a problem, then we know how to solve it ourselves next time. What other strategies could we use?"

Prompts that help children internalize these options also make them more portable. For example, when a child encounters a problem, asking, "What can you do?" has several benefits. It reminds the student of her agency—"I can do something"—and asks for an exploration of possibilities without actually insisting that they are tried. It's a very different prompt from "Sound it out" or "What would make sense there?" in that it requires the child to be in control of the exploration and selection of strategies, not just the exercise of them. This is part of teaching toward the development of "inner control," freeing the strategy use from the teacher's support.[14] The same is true of the prompt, "How could you solve this problem?" which asks for a potential plan of action and makes people more optimistic.[15]

❦ *"How are you planning to go about this?"*

Planning means organizing for a productive narrative. It's the most conscious part of being strategic since it happens before we get into the middle of things. It's a very agentive thing to do. Notice that the way this particular question is asked assumes that of course the student already has a plan. Some students, not having a plan or having even considered the possibility of planning, will find the question slightly puzzling, but will generate a possible plan and begin thinking about what it would take to enact it. However, planning is not always approached as directly as this. For example, "We will want to check our science experiments and check our math today. How much time do you think you'll need to finish your research projects this morning?" This at once models planning (planning is something we do all the time in this class), gives the children choice over their use of time (while not over what needs to be done) and requires them to mentally engage in the task analysis that is essential to planning. It really invites them to co-construct a plan for the rest of the afternoon. Planning is imagining a possible agentive narrative which can later be rehearsed through "How did you...?" and "Did your plan help you?"

❧ *"Where are you going with this piece [of writing]?"*
This question, like the previous one, is about planning and is forceful because there is no way to answer it simply without accepting the premise that you are in fact going somewhere with it—you have a goal, and possibly a plan. A child faced with the question might not yet have considered the possibility that going somewhere with a piece of writing is something one does. The question opens space for imagining such a possibility and in the longer term for acting in that way. It also opens the next step in the agentive conversation, such as, "What are you going to do next to get there?"

❧ *"Which part are you sure about and which part are you not sure about?"*
This question, addressed to a student who was aware he had spelled a word unconventionally, redirected his attention to the successful part of his efforts and then focused his problem-solving on the unsolved part, making the problem more focused and thus more tractable. Followed by, "How else could you spell that part?" he was able to try options and then recognize the correct version, thus successfully spelling the word. Following this with "How did you figure that out?" would invite an agentive narrative and a rehearsal of the strategy used.

The "Which part are you sure about?" is yet another version of drawing attention to the partially successful and reminds us that the experience of success necessary for developing a sense of agency is partly a matter of perception. Two children might misspell the same word and one will view it as a success and the other as a failure depending on whether they focus on the erroneous or accurate part of the spelling, the process they used to arrive at the spelling, or whether they focus on the fact that the word had the desired effect on the reader. The language we choose in our interactions with children will influence the ways they frame these events, and the ways the events influence their developing sense of agency and competence.

❧ *"You really have me interested in this character [in your writing] because of the things he says, and if you show me how he says them and what he looks like I will get an even stronger sense of him..."*
This statement is, again, drawing the child's attention first, and specifically, to what has gone well. In particular, though, it shows what

went well through its *effect* on the audience, showing the agency of authorship. This gets around the need for praise, which can build dependencies, and allows developing writers to understand how to tell for themselves whether their efforts were or will be successful.

However, pointing out to a student what worked well is not enough. Teaching requires moving beyond that to what is next for the student's development. Knowing the importance of this second step, we are inclined to say, "You really have me interested in this character [in your writing] because of the things he says, but you haven't..." In this construction, the one word, *but*, effectively undermines the first piece of feedback. It's the *and* in the first part of the quote that is critical. Notice how not only is the causal affirmation in the first part left intact, but the remainder of the sentence is likely to be "...and if you... then..." In other words, this structure sets up a possible future, including an audience consequence, a strategy that leads to it, and a narrative with the student as agentive protagonist. The one word, *and*, changes the entire structure of the interaction, affecting the motive for engaging the feedback and the implications for the child's identity.

This is not to ignore the value of "*but*," which has a different function, one of presenting a conflict for resolution. For example, responding to a child's misreading of *went*, a teacher might say "*went* would make sense (affirmation), but what letters would you expect if it were *went?*" Such prompts are intended to pose a problem for the learner to solve, often requiring some reorganization of cognitive processing.[16] Notice, though, that the affirmation still comes first. Notice, too, that while the affirmation has some of the qualities of praise, it's quite different. It attributes the source of the productive aspect to a warrant (makes sense) that the child is assumed to have used. Whether or not the child used the warrant, the retelling implies it in a way that makes the attribution difficult to reject. Actually, warrants like this are a critical part of persuasive storytelling, and some children need serious persuasion to desert their old unproductive stories. Perhaps you have come across this in parts of your own life.

I shouldn't leave the quote without also describing the importance of *if* ("and if you..."). There is a difference in a writing conference between saying, "If you were to add information about the cat, where would you put it?" and, "Put in more information about the cat."[17] One leaves open the choice of actually doing it,

43
❧

but insists on rehearsing the thinking behind it (the important instructional piece) and the other leaves no choice—a reduction in autonomy and agency. In fact, the question and the imperative have very different implications for motive, agency, and identity.

❦ *"That's like Kevin's story. He started off telling us his character is a lonely boy to get us caring about the main character. You [looking at Kevin] made a conscious choice."*[18] The teacher paused in a read-aloud to connect the author's writing process to that of her student Kevin. The key word in the fragment is "choice." Choice is central to agency. Making a choice requires one to act—preferably to deliberate and act. Often, we do things in particular ways, or see things through particular perspectives, forgetting that there are options. The comment reminds Kevin, and the class, that authors make decisions and should consciously contemplate them. Connecting the student's work to that of a published author whose work the students admire, clearly announces Kevin as an author. It invites the class to treat Kevin as an author and to break down any barriers between other, more published authors and authors like Kevin. While valorizing Kevin as an author, this is not simply "praise." It's information provided in a way that makes public recognition possible without some of its side effects. In public settings praise for an individual always runs the risk of "unpraising" others. "Good" can be praise but, following "wonderful" to another student, can be "faint praise."

The "choice" aspect of the comment also leads to a productive narrative about the choosing process. For example, "I notice you chose to write about this as a poem. How come?" insists on a narrative about the grounds for an authorial decision, requiring an articulation of something that might have been an unconscious process. At the same time, it requires the student to don an author's identity to give the narration, and opens a broader conversation with the class regarding choices among genres, and the grounds for making such choices.

Choice is important to foreground in classroom interactions. It provides children with a sense of autonomy. Also, sometimes children behave in challenging ways, and one step in changing behavior for the long term is to remind them that their behavior reflects a choice, and to help them think through the alternatives and their consequences. Imagining making different choices helps a lot.

Sometimes, children don't see something as a choice because they can't imagine the options. It's just something that they do. This is when we pose "Suppose..." or "What if..." possibilities for them, or open new possibilities by connecting them to other sources. For example, we might ask, "How would [familiar author, respected other, etc.] handle this?" "How about [another familiar author, respected other, etc.]...?" Rachel White and her colleagues showed that, if before young children engage in a task, they are asked, "What would Batman do?" they perform better.[19] This is partly because the question gives some perspective distance between the self and the task, and partly because (at least with adults) taking up an identity that has expectations of competence (doctor, scientist) also improves performance.[20] These questions not only turn children's attention to the need for conscious choice, but also to possible sources for imagining options.

❦ *"Why..."*

Why questions are the essence of inquiry. Once young children latch onto why questions they come to see how useful they are for getting to the bottom of how (some) things work. Aside from being the basis of at least one side of science and logic, why questions also develop persuasion and argumentation abilities, and logical thinking.

We can also apply "why" to aspects of human behavior. Questions like: "Why might [author name] choose to do that?"[21] ask students to view writing as fundamentally intentional and rife with decisions. Naturalizing such conversations provides grounds for critical literacy. It opens the possibility of considering word choice, ideology, and private interest as important considerations when reading. It also requires children, as readers, to imagine themselves into the writer's role, building a bridge between reading and writing that helps to generalize what is learned in one to become useful in the other. Imagining why an author made particular choices opens the possibility of doing things differently, so we can ask, "How else could she [the author] have done that?"

Of course, this can also be asked with respect to the student's own writing as, "How could you have done that differently?" Both together build the necessary links between reading and writing. "Why did the author choose that word?" "What other words could she have used?" "Do you think when she used that word to describe

45
❦

[a character], it changed the way we thought about him?" are all part of a systematic effort to insist that students take the intentionality and political nature of authorship as a given. Once established, this empowers children to read against the author's intentions. It becomes possible and more likely for them to read critically. Within these conversations, children can start to imagine what a writer has systematically left out—voices, perspectives, details—and to exercise control over their reading.

We can ask why characters behaved as they did, which will expand the children's mind reading ability, which we will take up in Chapter 7. However, why questions are less helpful in solving emotionally laden social friction in the classroom. For example, when children find themselves in a fight, asking why one hit the other will likely get a response that includes problematic attributions and further emotion. Better to first acknowledge the combatants' emotions so they can recognize them and don't have to further invest in them, and then ask, "What's the problem?" After hearing the participants' perspectives, we can offer a description of the problem which gives a little psychological distance and can be stated in a way that's something they have agreed upon. Now we have a problem that's not personalized, and is potentially solvable. We can invite possible solutions, suggesting options as necessary, and finally offer them an agentive narrative they can live with: "You figured out what the problem was and how to solve it yourselves. A lot of grownups don't know how to do that."

Powerful Narratives

The concept of agency in literacy and learning is important for the individual's sense of competence and well-being, and for their academic performance.[22] It's also indispensable to democratic living, though an individual sense of agency is not enough for that. As we shall see in Chapter 9, both individual and collective agency are important to develop because there are many situations in which an individual alone cannot solve a problem or have influence. Collective agency offers the individual sense of agency plus the joint sense of agency that can carry with it its own rewarding emotions along with developing a sense of belonging through the affiliative action. ~~Have a nice day!~~ Make it a nice day!

Extension

Analyze the following transcripts in terms of their invitations to agency and see whether there are ways to enhance them.

Transcript 1

Bill: You worked hard on this page. Where was the tricky part? (The student points to the word *through*.) Look at the picture and tell me what she did.
Peter: She went over the fence.
Bill: It could be *over*, but check to see if what you read looks right.
Peter: No, it's not *over*.
Bill: How do you know?
Peter: There's no *v*.
Bill: Good checking. What would make sense?
Peter: I don't know.
Bill: Would *through* make sense?
Peter: Oh, yeah—"through the fence."

Transcript 2

Kathy: Today's story is called *Cat on the Mat*. Look at the last word in the title; that word is the same as your name, isn't it?
Matt: I don't know.
Kathy: Sure it is, your name is Matt, isn't it? And this word is *mat*, except this word only has one *t* instead of two *t*'s like in your name. I will read you the story and you read along. "The cat sat on the mat. The goat sat on the mat. The cow sat on the mat. The elephant sat on the mat. SSppstt." [The sound of the cat scaring off the others] Can you sound out those letters?
Matt: [Trying to sound out SSppstt] *sssss. Tttt*
Kathy: Good. I'll finish the book now: "The cat sat on the mat."

Both these transcripts are from the excellent book: *Partners in Learning: Teachers and Children in Reading Recovery*.[23] Although there are some productive examples of teacher talk in the first transcript, both examples are shown in the book to be problematic. The first is problematic because the teacher did not realize that Peter had lost track of characters and thought that *she* referred to the fox. The second is problematic because of the text/task difficulty and because of the teacher's conception of reading instruction—what she was trying to do. She was trying to get the student to recognize and sound out words that were beyond her student's present capability rather than trying to arrange for him to take control of reading the book.

Meaning-Making Mindsets

Children who think they don't know how to write don't really need spelling lessons, at least not at first. They need to learn not to be afraid to try.

Katie Wood Ray & Lisa Cleaveland[1]

What makes children afraid to try? An answer to this question can be found in a study by Claudia Mueller and Carol Dweck in which they had fifth-grade students take an easy test then explained to half of them, individually, "This is your score. It's a very good score. You must be smart at this."[2] The other half were told, "This is your score. It's a very good score. You must have worked hard." They then offered the students the opportunity to choose a test they would like to take if there was time at the end, one that was "easy like the first one" or one that was "hard, but you might learn something from it." Better than 90 percent of the students who "must have worked hard" chose the challenging opportunity to learn. However, only about a third of the "you must be smart at this" students chose that option, two thirds being afraid to try. But that's not all. They all took a hard test and then a final easy test like the first one, and on the easy test, the "worked hard" students improved their performance over the initial test. The "smart" students' performance deteriorated. Offered the opportunity to take some problems home to work on, the "worked hard" students were interested, the "smart" students, not so much. Finally, given the chance to write down their test score, 40 percent of the "smart" students lied, inflating their score, even though nobody they knew would ever see the score. The "worked hard" group didn't feel that need to lie.

The reason a single piece of feedback has such extensive effects is that it awakened an entire meaning-making system. "You must be smart" induced students to think that people are interested in whether or not they are smart, a characteristic they think is a fixed character trait and one that can be deduced from a single test performance. Given that set of beliefs, a *fixed mindset*, their goal becomes validating their ability—looking smart. To do so, they avoid challenges that might produce errors or low performance, and any suggestion they put effort into it, both of which, within that belief system, would indicate low ability. These students don't persist when they encounter difficulty both because it would offer more evidence of low ability and because encountering difficulty makes them doubt their own ability to be successful.[3] Sometimes it becomes necessary to lie, cheat, or blame something or someone else in order to maintain an impression of high ability. It's easy to see how within this meaning-making system, children might be afraid to try. If you ask children with this fixed mindset "When do you feel smart?" they'll say something like when they don't make mistakes or when they finish their work quicker than others or when they do better than others.[4]

What about the "You must have worked hard" students? They were invited into a different system of beliefs, goals, and feelings—a growth mindset. For them, ability is not a fixed property because working hard can grow it. More learning becomes their goal. When they encounter difficulty, they can redouble their effort, encouraging a sense of agency. In this *growth mindset* learning has special significance as a goal because it offers the opportunity for growth. Errors and approximations are seen as normal parts of the learning process, not to be feared, but to be embraced as sources of information. Working hard is valued because it's likely to lead to more learning. When you ask students with this growth mindset when they feel smart, they respond with instances such as when they're working on solving difficult problems or when they're using what they know to teach others.

I don't want to suggest that attributing success to effort and failure to insufficient effort is a universally useful option. Far from it. Effort is simply part of the process. If a student is trying their hardest and still failing, redoubling efforts is clearly not the answer. In fact, suggesting increased effort in that circumstance will backfire and invite attention to a fixed ability mindset. Rather than added effort, trying new strategies would be more productive.

Small differences in our language invoke these mindsets, structuring beliefs, goals, and behaviors with far-reaching consequences.[5] The consequences are most powerful when children encounter difficulty. For example, when Andrei Cimpian and his colleagues gave young children person-oriented feedback ("You're a good drawer") or process feedback ("You did a good job drawing") on their artwork, it made no obvious difference when they were being successful.[6] But when they encountered difficulty, the ones who had previously received person-oriented positive feedback felt less positive about their art, about themselves as artists, and even about themselves as people, and they were less likely to choose to do art in the future. Children receiving the process-oriented feedback were less affected by these disabling feelings. And that's even with relatively unhelpful process feedback. Imagine the difference with feedback that focused on specific strategies the child used.

These mindsets and interventions based on them have been heavily studied.[7] A growth mindset is associated with greater resilience and a fixed mindset is associated with more helpless responses.[8] And mindsets are related to achievement, especially among average and below achieving students and minorities.[9] I hope this little introduction provokes the question, "How do we shift children's mindsets toward growth?"

Glad you asked.

Inviting a Growth Mindset

The first way to reduce the likelihood of a fixed mindset is to ensure that children are engaged. When they are fully engaged, children become the activity. Other worries, like how they look, tend to be forgotten, at least for the moment. They become the activity. In literacy, this can be accomplished when children have a range of accessible, personally relevant books, meaningful projects like making books, a degree of autonomy, time, and easy access to support.[10] But our language is important too.

🌱 *"See how you two worked that out by yourselves? Jamal, you just had to explain to your partner what the problem was and why it was a problem."*
Susie Althof gave this feedback to two of her kindergarten students who she had just shepherded through the process of resolving an interpersonal conflict. The first part of her comment leaves the two students with a positive identity as the kind of people who can solve problems together—and a sense of agency. Her assertion is a bit of a historical stretch given that they needed a lot of support in the shepherding process. But her concern is with how they *remember* what happened, what they can learn from the event. So, with her eye on the next time they encounter a problem (and they will) she reminds them of how the resolution was accomplished.

Helping children acquire a sense of agency in figuring out how to solve social problems like this reduces the disruptions to their academic learning while helping them to build healthy relationships, and prophylactically saving a bunch of future marriages, friendships, and business partnerships. But the agentive process narrative Susie offers is at the heart of the growth mindset. It draws the focus away from performance goals and interpersonal comparisons and focuses on strategies. Everything I described in the chapter on agency is relevant for building a growth mindset. I won't repeat that detail here.

🌱 *"Maybe you should find another way to do it."*
In a study by Melissa Kamins and Carol Dweck, this process-oriented feedback was given to some kindergartners in response to a pretend error.[11] Other children were given the person-oriented response, "I'm disappointed in you." When both groups subsequently role-played making a mistake in their pretend art work and receiving neutral feedback—"That house has no windows"—their ratings of their experience were quite different. Those who had previously experienced the process-oriented criticism felt positive about the experience, rated their art work positively, felt smart and good, and when asked what they would do next offered ways they could fix the problem. Children who had previously received the

person-oriented feedback had the opposite experience. They rated their art work a full standard deviation lower than the process group, did not feel positive about the experience, and didn't feel smart or good. Instead of role-playing constructive strategies, they role-played helpless behavior and crying.

Person-oriented criticism is not a good idea. However, it turns out that person-oriented praise is no better. Repeating the study with praise had the same effects. "I'm proud of you," "You're good at this," "Good boy" all effectively invoke a fixed mindset, negative feelings about self and competence, and helpless responses.[12] Unfortunately, adults tend to give more, and more exaggerated, person-oriented praise to children with lower self-esteem.[13] When you receive this kind of praise, you know at least that people are judging you as a person.

Maybe we should find another way to do it.

"Yet"

The word "yet" is key to shifting toward growth theorizing. If a student says, "I'm not good at this," you respond, "*yet...* I'm not good at this *yet*. Let's think about how we could become better at this." This frames competence in terms of growth, something over which the student has control. College students receiving feedback that they had not mastered the course material *yet* were more likely to adopt a growth mindset, to feel encouraged, and to assume their teacher held a growth mindset than were students whose feedback did not include the word "yet."[14] "Yet" offers the possibility of change.

This is probably too obvious to mention, nonetheless, moving children toward a growth mindset means avoiding language like "You always..." or "You never..." which speak clearly to the fixedness of whatever behavior is referred to. (I advise also avoiding this within committed relationships.)

❧ *"What does it mean when we make a mistake?"*
Used to this narrative, Susie's kindergartners chorused, "We fix it!" Acknowledging their response, Susie explained that if we weren't making mistakes, we wouldn't be challenging ourselves and wouldn't be learning. "Mistakes are where we learn." She asked them whether

they thought that Barack Obama (president at the time) made mistakes when he was in kindergarten. They all agreed that he probably did. If even Susie and Barack Obama made mistakes, well, a growth mindset is imminent.

🌱 *"Remember the first week when we had to really work at walking quietly? Now you guys do it automatically."*[15]
Recognizing that change is possible is central to a growth mindset. You only need to believe that change is possible, not that it can be huge or easy. So we take opportunities to point out to students their change over time, their learning history. Showing children how they have changed as community members, learners, readers, and writers, reveals that they are in the process of becoming. This category of questions includes ones like "How have you changed as a writer?" and "What do you think you need to work on next?" and comments like "Look what you were doing back in January. Look how far you've come." Building into classroom practice self-assessments, reviewing at the end of a lesson, day or week what students have learned—what they're doing now that they couldn't do before—also helps them recognize that change, and reduces the likelihood of their taking up a fixed mindset.

Drawing attention to change in learning and behavior allows children to project learning futures. Once children have a sense that they're constantly learning, and are presented with evidence of that historical growth, teachers can ask about their learning futures, and the plans they have for managing those futures. A sense of historical growth is a foundation for hope and optimism and, crucially, for a growth mindset.

A word should also be said here about the teacher's use of *"guys."* In English, we lack a neutral second-person plural pronoun. *Guys* has evolved to be largely gender-neutral in common use—witness here (and in several other places) a female teacher using it thus.[16] Nonetheless, many hear it as part of a larger network of male-default sounding terms like *chairman, manmade, mankind,* and *man the pumps,* and thus oppressive. Some might argue that it's not that bad because many -*man*- words are from the Latin root meaning *hand.* But many are not, and besides, the problem is how words *feel* to hearers. Just calling a mixed-gender group "gals" should make this evident. Fortunately, in the classroom we can solve the problem with words like: Everyone, people, folks, scholars, friends, fellow researchers, mathematicians, team, colleagues, classmates, or you all (or y'all).

❦ *"He just made a bad choice, don't you think?"*

But it isn't just learning over which students have some agency. They need to realize they have agency in who they become—what sort of person. We make that clear with comments like, "I see you're *choosing* to be the kind of person who notices when... and acts to make things right." When Pegeen Jensen was reading aloud to her first graders, one of them pointed to a character saying, "He's a bad boy." Pegeen immediately responded, "He just made a bad choice, don't you think?" We avoid good/bad person binaries. Rather than saying "That's what good readers do" we can say, "That's what readers do," and we can say it whether it's about being strategic or making errors because those are both indeed what readers do. We also avoid categorical ability labels. Even comments like, "Joseph was called a math whiz" can invoke a fixed mindset in the classroom.[17]

❦ *"This is the book Rachel made. You must have worked hard on it for a long time, Rachel. What was the most difficult part of making your book?"*

It's good practice to celebrate children's work. It's also important for children to see that such accomplishments were a result of hard work and problem-solving. Within that frame, we can identify new creative features and decisions that Rachel made along the way. Without the attention to the effort and strategy, just celebrating the final product can lead to a fixed mindset, particularly if we only choose to present the most advanced work. Notice how the teacher's question emphasizes Rachel's authorship with "the book Rachel made" and "your book."

Children making books is a good example of a classroom environment that allows a growth mindset to flourish. This is not only because it's a meaningful and engaging activity, but also because it offers many different ways for children to competently participate in the literate community with no obvious way to invite interpersonal comparisons. A classroom with a narrow, mechanical view of reading (or math), with ability grouping, invites interpersonal comparisons on the valued competencies, and a fixed mindset, even if the teacher doesn't verbally draw those comparisons. Other unspoken nudges toward a fixed mindset in classrooms include persistently using the most advanced work as exemplars, giving privileges to higher achievers or for best work, or focusing on speed.

❧ *"Remember the other day when Janaya shared her story about [describes story]? Well, when Janaya went back to work yesterday, she did something else to help readers understand her story, kind of like what Jazmine did the other day. [Shows book.] She put some letters on her page to help readers like us understand her story. Right, here's a J."*[18] The teacher reminds the children that they don't have to start a new book each day as some tend to do in the beginning. At the same time, she is very specific about Janaya's *growth* and, because of the timeline, she makes it clear that the story took an extended period of time and effort. By adding "to help readers understand her story" she names Janaya's effort as strategic, and book making as an intentional social practice. The teacher offers adding print as a new avenue for growth in literacy development, as one of the many ways of demonstrating learning and competence in her classroom. She also opens the possibility of learning from peers—"kind of like what Jazmine did the other day"—and makes it clear that revision is normal in the classroom, which is also consistent with the actions of teachers who are good at developing growth mindsets.[19] Notice that although there is no actual praise, her comments are positive and Janaya will likely feel a measure of pride in her achievement and the work that went into it, and lean toward a growth mindset.

❧ *"That's not surprising, the confusion, because there are so many flashbacks that help us get to what the character is thinking."*[20] Ms. Tucker's response to Zion, her eighth-grade student's public confession of confusion during a read-aloud, rendered it normal, indeed, expected. The student's admission itself is evidence that the class fosters a growth mindset. He wouldn't express his confusion in a fixed mindset classroom because it would be seen as evidence of his lack of ability. It's Ms. Tucker's response, and others like it, that render his instructionally valuable admission possible. Her initial response is made even more powerful by a subsequent observation in which she casts confusion as a positive, even enjoyable state:

"Do you remember in *The Secret Story of Sonia Rodriguez*, how the inferences we made initially were wrong? We learned that when we kept reading. We were surprised at the end, and that was fun. We don't know yet." A history of these interactions also made possible a growth mindset response from another student regarding the flashbacks and confusion. He said, "I like that. It makes you think, and it makes you want to get into the book more. You don't want all the answers on one page. You want to think." On another occasion a different student, Shea, observed: "I'm like really, really confused… but it's, like, good." These responses indicate that the growth mindset is part of the culture of the classroom, which magnifies the power of Ms. Tucker's comments. Normalizing confusion further, Ms. Tucker herself occasionally admits to her own confusion and entertains her students' efforts to help out.

Notice also how Ms. Tucker capitalized on the opportunity offered by Zion's admission, to give a brief lesson on flashbacks as part of helping students learn how to deal with such text complexities. She makes it clear that students are not on their own in their learning, pointing out that, "We'll figure out how to do this together." When students are struggling, we don't want them to think the burden is entirely on them. They need to know that we have their backs, that one option for moving forward is to seek help. Indeed, one of the students, Kendall, observed: "We have all these teachers to help us… They tell us, like, 'Well I'll help you with this book.'"

🌱 *"I know getting stuck on a problem like this can be frustrating, but let's see what we know already."*
Just as recognizing confusion is a normal part of learning, teachers who are good at building a growth mindset in their classrooms tend to recognize the feelings associated with encountering difficulties, including the negative ones.[21] At the same time, this comment sets up a strategy for moving forward, and because of the "we," makes it clear that the student is not alone in figuring out this new learning.

🌱 *"Failures and errors are valuable. They're where we learn. How can we learn from this?"*
How we (teachers and parents) respond to children's errors and failures has a big impact on children's mindset development. Parents who address children's failures as valuable parts of learning, not

something that impairs learning and growth, tend to have children who develop growth mindsets. Parents primed to view failures as obstacles to development start to engage in person-oriented thinking and behaviors that lead to a fixed mindset. For example, they worry that their child isn't good at the subject, try to comfort the child and explain that not being the most talented is okay.[22]

Long Tentacles

The growth mindset essentially assumes that the self, with all its intellectual and other qualities, is learning, growing, and open to strategic change. It implies a self that is potentially self-authoring within the vicissitudes of circumstance. A fixed mindset implies that personal qualities are unchanging character traits, and that behaviors are indicators of those traits. In the fixed mindset there is no agency over self-construction, only over the performance of the (fixed) self. Consequently, these mindsets have long tentacles that reach into many corners of social, emotional, and moral development (see a summary in Table 5.1).[23]

Consider this. Some people think that prejudice is a fixed property of individuals. These people, regardless of how prejudiced they are, worry most about looking prejudiced to themselves and others.[24] They are not interested in engaging in interracial interactions and diversity experiences, which might make them look prejudiced. And when they do engage, they show greater anxiety than those who view prejudice as a malleable feature. Even in matters of diversity, we want to invoke a growth mindset, making clear to students that people's behavior is a result of their thoughts and feelings, which can be changed. As teachers, our job is to pass on the accumulated tools of humanity while supporting the evolution of society. If we want an inclusive, learning society, we need to help children develop the tools to create that society. Those tools include experiences with productive interracial collaboration and the language practices that made them possible.

It's not difficult to see how some of the consequences shown in the table are linked. For example, within a growth mindset, understanding other people's behavior requires understanding their thoughts, feelings, and context. In a fixed mindset, others' behaviors are simply evidence of character traits (smart, courageous, evil).

Table 5.1 Consequences of Growth and Fixed Mindsets

Growth Mindset	Fixed Mindset
Choose challenging activities in which they will learn as much as possible. Get into their zone of proximal development.[25]	Choose activities that make them look smart—easy enough to be successful but not quite difficult enough to make errors and learn.
When encountering difficulty, they engage in self-monitoring and self-instruction, increase strategic efforts, and don't see self as failing.	When encountering difficulty, view the difficulty as failure, question their ability, assign blame for failure, and cease acting strategically.
Linked to higher achievement, especially among average and below students.	Linked to lower achievement, especially among average and below students.[26]
Encountering difficulty or having to work hard have no effect on sense of competence.[27]	Encountering difficulty or having to work hard lowers sense of competence.
Feel smart when taking on challenges or teaching others.	Feel smart when doing things better or faster than others.
What advice would they give to a peer who is having difficulty? Lots of strategic advice.	Advice offered a peer who is having difficulty would be minimal and perhaps accompanied by sympathy.
Explain behaviors in terms of mental processes and context.	Explain behaviors in terms of permanent traits.
What do they make of a new child in class who misbehaves (or does badly on work)? Probably not a bad student; probably better in a couple of weeks.	Probably a bad student; probably much the same in a couple of weeks.

(Continued)

Table 5.1 (*continued*)

Growth Mindset	Fixed Mindset
When faced with transgressions, try to understand the thinking and the context that produced the behavior, and forgive and educate the transgressor. Lean toward restorative justice.[28]	When faced with transgressions, invoke punishment.
When faced with disagreements in the process of learning: Engage the disagreement and try to synthesize the views. Enhance view of partner in the process.[29]	Turn the disagreement into a relational confrontation. Put partner down.
Slow to judge and form stereotypes. More interested in neutral or conflicting information.[30]	Judge quickly and form stereotypes. Focus on information confirming stereotype. Ignore disconfirming information.
Older students think education is to help people understand the world and to prepare them for socially useful work.[31]	Older students think the purpose of education is to enhance wealth and socioeconomic status.
High school students are less interested in social status relevant characteristics. Less willing to use relational aggression (exclusion, ostracism, rumors, etc.) to maintain status.[32]	High school students are highly attentive to social status relevant characteristics. More willing to use relational aggression to maintain status.

Table 5.1 (*continued*)

Growth Mindset	Fixed Mindset
Less vulnerable to depressive thinking. View these and difficulties as signals to act.	More vulnerable to depressive and suicidal thinking, and allow it to affect their personal and academic lives. Difficulties produce a downward spiral.[33]
More likely to have friendship relationships with qualities of trust, mutual sharing of difficulties and adaptive problem-solving.[34]	Relationships less likely to have these qualities.

Their thoughts and feelings are not particularly relevant. This in turn has implications for relationships and for moral judgments. For example, with a fixed mindset, disagreements easily lead to relational conflict and putting one's partner down, in order to protect one's sense of competence. Only one person can be right and thus smart. With a growth mindset, partners work to synthesize opposing views and elevate their opinion of their partner's ability.

Within a fixed mindset, misbehavior invokes punishment. A growth mindset leads to education and restorative justice because people's behavior is dependent on their thoughts, beliefs, feelings, and context which can be changed. This is also one reason why we ask questions like "What is she thinking?" and "How do you think they feel about that?" regarding peers and characters in books, conversations we will explore further in Chapter 7. This also coincides nicely with asking students to explain their thinking whether they have solved a problem correctly or incorrectly, so that students' attention is drawn to the thinking explanation and the possibility of change, rather than a fixed character trait explanation.

Flexibility and Transfer (or Generalizing)

Is there a way to come to understand the world that does not simultaneously set the stage for limited use of that knowledge?

Ellen Langer and Alison Piper[1]

A colleague tells a story about his daughter learning to write. Her teacher tells him in a conference that she is doing badly writing in school. My colleague protests that she writes wonderfully at home, however the teacher shows him examples of her school writing that, he concedes, confirm the teacher's view. He takes the matter up with his daughter who is genuinely surprised that the two activities are related in any way. What she knows about writing at home does not seem at all relevant to school writing. I have certainly had this experience with children, especially in math. Strategies used to calculate area for a math quiz seem to have no relevance when faced with a problem of calculating garden space. Children often know things from their writing that they fail to use when solving problems in reading. The stories they tell in these different life spaces are different—different genres, settings, characters, and goals.

These are problems of transfer—the failure to generalize learning from one situation to another. Teachers and other researchers of all stripes have puzzled over this problem for a long time. However, in some classrooms children quite flexibly generalize what they have learned. For example, in one classroom in which children had been using the strategy of "stepping into" characters, taking their perspective, one of the children did this in science as they studied ducklings. He hypothesized about the basis for the duckling's behavior by taking the duckling's perspective. When he did this, another child, used to looking for such parallels, noticed and pointed out to the class what he had done. It seems that the less compartmentalized we make children's learning lives, the more likely they are to transfer their strategic problem-solving to other situations. These children were also flexible in the ways they applied strategies in order to solve a given problem. Rather than inflexibly repeating the same strategy, or quitting, they were likely to use multiple strategies. What makes this possible? How do teachers build bridges between activity settings, making it so that the agency a child exercises in writing transfers to her reading or math? How do they get a child to apply strategies flexibly and in new situations? Or perhaps the question is: How do we prevent children from knowing things in a fixed and rigid fashion?

Actually, a lot of the conversations we have already discussed have implications for flexibility and transfer. For example, encouraging children to entertain certain identities can help. Consider this. A study compared the arithmetic learning of shopkeepers with that of high school students apprenticed to shopkeepers in an adult education class.[2] Which group would you predict to be more successful? It turns out that the shopkeepers were more successful at transferring their learning to their out-of-class shopkeeping lives most likely because in both situations they had the same goal or problem: How to make their business more profitable. The high school students, on the other hand, had different goals in the two settings: Acquiring knowledge in one setting, generating a profit in the other. This same logic would help explain why children who learn words for their spelling test commonly don't transfer the learning to their writing. Once children incorporate into their identities a sense that they are writers doing writerly things (or scientists, mathematicians, etc.) they can ask themselves in a new situation (not necessary consciously) what they might do *as a writer,* since those roles do not stop at the border of a single activity setting. We might point that out to them with comments like, "When you're at home in bed tonight and not quite asleep, you might think of something you want to add to your book tomorrow, because writers don't just think about their writing when they're at their desks." Imagining oneself as the writer of a piece can also help transfer writing experience to one's activities as a reader.

In Chapter 4, I noted the value of asking "How did you...?" normalizing children articulating their strategies to their teacher and each other. This strategy has an additional advantage. Bethany Rittle-Johnson and her colleagues asked some four- and five-year-olds to explain to their mothers how they solved a puzzle.[3] The mother listened but didn't respond. Another group were asked to explain their strategy just to themselves, and a third group were not asked to explain. When a new situation called for the strategy, children who had explained to a listener, even one who didn't respond, were more able to transfer the strategy to the new context. But there are more ways in which teacher talk serves to encourage transfer and flexibility.

❦ *"One of the things people do when they start a story is think of what they know. Mathematicians do this too... Let's try it."*[4]

Reminding children to begin a new activity by taking stock of what they already know has several functions. First, it reduces the magnitude of the problem to be solved. Second, it puts the new problem in the context of old, already solved problems. Third, it opens the possibility of more connections among the new knowledge and what is already known. However, this particular invitation takes a couple of extra steps. It represents the problem-space of readers as similar to that of mathematicians, encouraging active transfer of a strategy across what would otherwise have seemed to be quite different activities. The ability to solve new problems flexibly depends on how the problem is viewed in the first place— whether the strategic demands are seen as similar to other, familiar problems.[5] The invitation encourages children to increase the boundaries within which they look for problem similarities, stretching beyond the surface structure of activities to more metaphorical levels. The "let's" is also important. Collaborative problem-solving offers more perspectives that can help with re-framing. More on this later.

❦ *"How could we use what we just learned?"*

Asking children to contemplate the use of new learning can lead them to think through possibilities and become more likely to actually use it. This applies to new strategies or concepts learned, but also more broadly. For example, oftentimes we read a book in which we learn about a problem or injustice and we close the book and move on. But what then is the point of having read the book? After reading *One Smile*[6] with her second and third graders Merry Komar asked them: "How can you make an impact on others at school, at home, and in the community?" The conversations about this and other books they had read opened a class inquiry about a Community Outreach Center, which led to their idea to make hygiene kits for homeless people, which they did, an act that made a difference and brought them a sense of social and moral agency. It's the question, "Now you know, what are you going to do about it?"

❦ *"How else…"*

It's wonderful when a child solves a problem. We can then ask them to regale us with the story of how they solved it, building their sense of agency. Then we can ask how *else* they might have solved it. Doing so sustains the possibility of choice (and thus agency) at the same time as maintaining a sense of flexibility—there's always another way. Even with less successful experiences it's possible, after pointing out what part did go well, to consider options with questions like, "Is there anything you might do differently?" emphasizing choice retrospectively—like revising and editing. Such questions are a bit risky though. They require a secure relationship within which exploration of past decisions is interesting and not grounds for blame.

"Else" is a very powerful word. At the same time as building flexibility, it implies a range of other important messages. For example, "How else could the author have said that?" not only builds flexibility, but also reminds students that writing is always intentional and, implicitly, that it's consequential. To bring the implicit reminder forward we might ask how saying it that way would change a reader's interpretation. In a similar way, "What else do you think [the audience] would like to know?" opens possibilities for inclusion in a piece of writing, but at the same time it reminds the young writer of his responsibilities to his audience. It's also a reminder that writers always make choices about what they include and exclude from their writing—what they choose to tell and not tell. Taking this concept back to children's reading opens a central conversation for critical literacy: What is the author not telling us? Whose perspectives are not represented? and so forth.

❦ *"That's like..."*

Aside from an expression of appreciation, the word "like" has two primary functions. It draws attention to connections (with other experiences, books, authors, situations, practices, words, and so forth) and it makes metaphors, both of which are fundamental not only to transfer, but also to understanding and reasoning. Connections are at the heart of comprehension. They provide anchors and retrieval routes. The more connections, the more flexibly something can be accessed.

Transfer involves overcoming apparent dissimilarities between activities. For example, reading web pages and reading a book are sufficiently different to limit the extent to which children might transfer what they have learned to do in one to their activities in the other. The same might be said of different genres of writing or of reading and writing. Increasing transfer primarily involves simply overcoming these apparent dissimilarities and encouraging children to ask in what ways one activity, problem, or role, is like another. This means thinking beyond the literal to the metaphorical, and the word *like* is very good for invoking metaphors. We want children to ask themselves not only "What do I know about this?" but "What do I know that is like this?"

At the same time as thinking metaphorically helps with transfer, it has other benefits. Metaphors provide new ways of understanding and deepening meaning, "stand[ing] with one foot in the known, while placing the other in the unknown." They are what Judith Lindfors calls "reaching devices."[7] For example, teaching about parallel circuits, June Williamson explains that "electricity finds another way to go. Kind of like when you're caught in traffic: Sometimes you can find another path around the jam."[8] A series circuit she likens to the World Series, "One game after another. And if you lose a game, you're out."

Indeed, Brian Sutton-Smith refers to the mind as fundamentally *multi-metaphoric*, observing that young children are very competent with metaphoric thought.[9] He points out that, "once children can speak, they move endlessly through the vocalized plural play of metaphor." As an example, he reports watching his two-year-old granddaughter playing in a sandpit, "first pouring the sand and calling it coke, and then rounding it and calling it an egg, and then lengthening the shape and calling it a sausage, and then banging and slapping it with a vocalized rhythm which she called a song, and so on. The properties of the material in the child's hands were 'poured' through a vocal string of metaphoric signifiers." Along with Gregory Bateson, Sutton-Smith argues that metaphor is essential to the evolution of thought, which advances by locating similarities among forms—how they are alike.[10]

The word *like* has other incidental properties too. When applied to people it emphasizes our common humanity over our individual and cultural uniquenesses and is thus productive in terms of building a caring, tolerant community. However, because *like* draws comparisons, it also raises the possibility of noticing contrasts, absences, and disjunctures. These are the crucial foundations not only of problem-formation and learning, but of critical literacy. We can ask about similarity and difference in the treatment of others, for example.

❧ "Could be" (vs. "is").

One thing that reduces flexibility is presenting information as facts rather than as possibilities—*is* rather than *could be*. Ellen Langer and Alison Piper presented two groups of college students with some items: A piece of a dog's chew toy, a polygraph pen, and a hair dryer attachment.[11] They introduced one group to the items saying, "This is a…" A second group was introduced to them with, "This could be a…" Later, the students were put in a situation in which they could use the items to solve problems, but only if they thought about the items flexibly, outside of their labels, for example using the rubber chew toy as an eraser. Only the "could be" students could do this. Just adding the element of uncertainty frees the item from its name. On the other hand, we can block flexibility simply by using *is*.

Langer and her colleagues found that students introduced conditionally to information, even if through their reading, not only were able use the information more flexibly, but they also performed better on a memory test of the material. Langer points out that "An awareness of alternatives at the early stages of learning a skill gives a conditional quality to the learning, which... increases mindfulness"—the source of flexibility, creativity, and much more (as we shall see).[12] We might bear this in mind, for example, when teaching children about phonics, an important element of early literacy learning. English is full of irregularities, polyphonic relationships and other complexities (e.g., have/gave, ear/bear, own/down, cough/through/though/thought, the y in yes/ by/baby, or live as a verb or adjective). Consequently, children need to expect that their first attempts at figuring out words using phonic relationships might not work. They need to apply the relationships flexibly, making sure their attempts make sense in the context. Teaching those relationships as rules and limiting exposure to complexities is likely to lead to inflexible use of phonics knowledge.

Kindergarten teacher Sarah Helmer held a ten-minute session on environmental print just before snack time. A child would bring in a piece of print found at home, like a cereal or soap box top. While the child stuck it to a chart and wrote their name next to it, Sarah invited the other children together to figure out the word using whatever strategies they had. Sarah would explain each strategy and invite or add others. During snack, I noticed that at one table a girl eating yogurt noticed the print on the container and figured it out. Immediately she turned to her neighbor and showed him. He picked up his snack wrapper and, unable to figure it out turned to his other neighbor for help. They figured it out and his neighbor picked up her snack wrapper to do the same. Aside from the acquiring a flexible, generalized use of the strategies learned in formal and environmental print lessons, the children were attuned to noticing and acting on environmental print, at home and at school.

❦ *"What if...?"*

Thinking flexibly and metaphorically involves expanding the imagination, and what if questions insist on an imaginative act. They can be used to expand the contexts in which particular strategies might be used, or particular identities might hold sway. Because we can't routinely be presented with multiple contexts, we help children do mind experiments to think themselves into other situations and try out their strategies making the necessary accommodations. For example, after a child has told us how he managed to research the characters for his historical fiction piece we might ask, "What if you were writing a science report. Would any of these strategies help there?"

"What if..." and "suppose..." invitations also develop children's ability with hypothetical talk and abstract thinking. They are the foundation of mind experiments and help children understand the possibility of multiple versions of reality. These abilities are fundamental to both productive individual choice and to negotiating collaboratively productive meanings and solutions as is required for democratic living. At the same time, these questions develop children's argumentation skill, particularly because they invite "if... then..." statements and the thinking that lies behind them. "What if" questions used in the context of narrative can also develop children's understanding of narrative structure since the questions require construction of alternative possibilities using narrative logic.

These hypotheticals can be used to explore worlds, behaviors, and choices without real consequences. Don Graves pointed out that posing hypotheticals like "Suppose you were going to put some dialogue into this story. Where would you put it?" can produce the necessary learning without the resistance that might come from the anticipated effort needed to actually do it.[13] It opens the imaginative possibility, and accomplishes the necessary instruction without risk. Of course, once the possibility is imagined it can be tempting to actually do it.

Hypotheticals are the stuff of invention. They are also a useful way into critical literacy since they can provide a way of stepping out of the known and taken-for-granted. For example, in a discussion of the disparity in pay between male and female athletes, many children still find it perfectly reasonable. However, when asked, "What if your mother were an athlete..." most of the children suddenly find it unreasonable. Mind experiments like this can allow us to notice things that are otherwise too naturalized to be noticed, and help us use our experience to understand possible events we have not experienced.

❦ *[Playful language].*

I should not leave the topic of flexibility and transfer without a comment on playfulness. Language play takes the pressure off language and literate practice and invites experimentation with alternative practices and realities. Writers like Dr. Seuss, Allan Ahlberg, Chris Raschka, Jon Klassen, and Jon Scieszka clearly have understood this. Also books like *Du Iz Tak? Froodle, Nothing Rhymes with Orange, Chester van Chime Who Forgot How to Rhyme,* or *The Cat Who Wore a Pot on Her Head* embrace play with language. There are few better ways to draw children's attention to the structure of words and texts than through language play and parody. Freed of the burden of meaning, nonsense rhymes and the like reveal the internal structure of words as an object of interest rather than of labor. Parodies do the same at the text level.

I asked a student in Laurie McCarthy's first-second grade classroom about a book he was working on. One page opening was about pizzas, one about swords, one about emeralds, and so on. Asked the title of the book, he turned to the cover of *The Absolutely Random Book*, read with peels of glee. He had deliberately violated the unwritten rule "stay on topic" for its humorous effect. This from a boy who six weeks earlier rejected invitations to write. Brian Sutton-Smith observes that "laughter is the most primitive form of parody and satire by which the sanctity of established ways gets impugned. It is life's basic form of unofficial response."[14] In other words, it's a good vehicle for flexibly breaking rules and testing boundaries. Playfulness with language might also be indispensable for building critical literacy, but perhaps as importantly, it's probably good for the soul.

An additional benefit, as I mentioned at the outset, is that playfulness can develop children's interest in language. For example, having read William Steig's *The Amazing Bone* with students it becomes possible for me to add into my classroom vocabulary "As I live and flourish…" and to stop inappropriate behavior with "Have you no shame sir!" or, better, "You worm, you odoriferous wretch!" or even, "Yibbam sibibble!"[15] These latter can be used to admonish because children's awareness of the source makes their use funny, taking the personal edge off the reprimand. At the same time, it builds the children's vocabulary and their interest in language, and reminds them of an excellent resource for further language development.

A Longer Example

At this point, I think we should put some of the brief snippets of language into context, so let me give another elaborated example of a teacher–student interaction that pulls together much of what I have already presented. Consider this transcript of a writing conference which I have taken from an excellent book called *How's It Going?* by Carl Anderson.[16]

Carl: You know, Maya, you're just like a lot of writers who write memoirs. Like Jean Little, for example. You know that story from *Little by Little*, the one in which her classmates make fun of her because of her eyeglasses?

Maya: Yeah.

Carl: Both you and Jean Little packed several scenes into a single piece of writing. But Jean Little didn't just stretch the first scene and list the rest. She stretched most of the scenes, the scenes that really helped us understand what she went through. You could revise by trying to make your memoir more like the ones you've read in class so far this year. That's what I want you to try—picking one of these other scenes and stretching it like you stretched the birthday candles.

Maya: Okay.

Carl: Which one would you want to try?

Maya: Maybe... I kind of like it the way it is.

Carl: I can understand that. But I'm still going to challenge you to take a risk as a writer by trying out Jean Little's way of stretching several scenes. And if you decide you don't like what it does to your piece after trying it, that's okay... I nudge students to try things I think will help them grow as writers. So which scene do you want to stretch—the scavenger hunt, the sleeping routine, your mom tucking you in...

Maya: I think my mom tucking me in.

Carl: [starts her on a new piece of paper] I'll check in with you later in the period to see how it goes.

This conference is really quite forceful, but when Carl returns to Maya, she is very satisfied with the outcome and chooses to make use of the new writing she produced. See Table 6.1 for what I see as significant pieces of this conference.

Table 6.1 Analysis of Carl's Conference with Maya

Carl's Talk	Commentary
Maya, you're just like a lot of writers who write memoirs.	Carl offers a specific identity—authors who write memoirs. He names memoirs as a kind of writerly thing to notice.
Like Jean Little... that story from *Little by Little*, the one in which her classmates make fun of her because of her eyeglasses?	Carl uses a specific example to show that the identity claim is not empty praise. It also shows the parallel between the writing and the writers, but also between the two lives. *Like* also becomes more normalized as a way of talking and thinking.
Both you and Jean Little packed several scenes into a single piece of writing.	Carl extends the evidence for the identity and opens a possibility for Maya's life and text narratives, and establishes the equivalent epistemological authority. He names "scenes" as something to be noticed—analyzing the task.
But Jean Little didn't just stretch the first scene and list the rest. She stretched most of the scenes,	Carl articulates and names the process used by the mentor author and notes that it is one Maya has already used—further task analysis.
that really helped us understand what she went through.	Carl shows the consequences of the author's use of the process/strategy, and the agentive, intentional nature of writing.

Table 6.1 (*continued*)

Carl's Talk	Commentary
You could revise by trying to make your memoir more like the ones you've read in class so far this year.	Carl opens an agentive possibility for Maya's writing along with an identity challenge.
That's what I want you to try—picking one of these other scenes and stretching it like you stretched the birthday candles.	Using positional authority, Carl requires Maya to pick up the challenge, retelling the previous agentive narrative to maintain the sense of agency. The task analysis maintains choice and opens the possibility for later strategic planning in writing.
Which one would you want to try?	Carl offers choice, and thus agency in the process, but constrains the possible narratives.
I can understand that. But I'm still going to challenge you to take a risk as a writer by trying out Jean Little's way of stretching several scenes.	Offering recognition of Maya's expression of her own agency, Carl adds to his positional authority the challenge to the identity already offered. This is an offer of a narrative with a specific identity and a challenge to overcome. If she picks up this challenge, she cannot help but pick up the authorial identity. To the extent that the identity is inviting, the narrative is inviting.

(Continued)

Table 6.1 (*continued*)

Carl's Talk	Commentary
if you decide you don't like what it does to your piece after trying it, that's okay...	Carl offers Maya a narrative in which she can regain the agency he has temporarily taken away by limiting her choices.
I nudge students to try things I think will help them grow as writers.	Reminding Maya of his role as a teacher, Carl reminds Maya of her identity as a writer, but also "help them grow" indicates that she also has an agentive role in her growth.
So which scene do you want to stretch—the scavenger hunt, the sleeping routine, your mom tucking you in...	"So now that you have agency as a writer and a learner, how do you want to retell your life narrative?" Also, Carl offers specific choice, and hence agency. With the specificity is the recognition that he is interested in Maya's life details, strengthening his relational position and Maya's authority.
I'll check in with you later in the period to see how it goes.	In case Maya decides to abandon the offered narrative, Carl at once closes the door on the lesser narrative and shows interest in her personally and as a writer.

Perhaps it seems in places as though I am stretching the intentions and the implications. I don't believe so, but if even half of my inferences are true, repeating these discursive currents over and over each day cannot help but have a powerful effect, the more so because it's not only Carl who is applying this discursive pressure toward agentive narratives. Once these conversations become naturalized in the classroom—ways of talking and interacting that imply roles, relationships, positions, authority, agency, epistemology, topics of conversation, and expected identities—they also become part of children's conversations.

In this chapter and the previous ones, I have emphasized the kinds of conversation that encourage children to see themselves as agentive, and thus responsible. In part, this involves recognizing multiple ways of seeing and solving problems, and a certain relish in doing so. If we fail to accomplish this, it does not bode well for children once they leave the educational environment. It remains possible (perhaps even common) for learners to leave school believing that they know a great deal but yet unable think for themselves, not seeing themselves as active inquiring individuals. The more we help children build a sense of themselves as inquirers and problem-solvers, and the less they see boundaries between domains of inquiry, the more they are likely to generalize their learning into the world beyond school.

Even this is not enough. I want children to see themselves not only as inquiring individuals, but as part of a diverse community that inquires, whose members, through their active participation and diversity of perspective, contribute to each other's intellectual, social, and emotional growth. It's to this social and emotional growth that I will turn next because it forms the foundation for intellectual development to which it is inextricably linked.

Emotional and Social Life

Emotional skills trump standardized measures of intelligence in predicting academic and personal achievement.

Mary Helen Immordino-Yang[1]

When children are born, they don't experience the emotions we know as adults, only positive and negative sensations that vary in intensity.[2] They learn to make sense of their sensations through interactions with caretakers around emotionally charged events. They learn to discriminate among the wide range of culturally available emotions like anger, disappointment, sadness, and impatience. They also must learn how to manage their emotions, and whether and when to express them.[3] As they develop these skills, their social lives improve. It's easier to be friends with people who can manage and appropriately express their emotions. But their academic lives improve too, because learning new skills and even cooperative play require managing emotions like frustration. Consequently, when children are emotionally competent, their lives are better. Heck, everyone's lives are better. Of course, social life requires not only recognizing and managing one's own emotions, it also requires recognizing others' emotions. If we can't read others' emotions, we can't tell the difference between sarcasm, banter, and support. We can't communicate effectively.

As teachers, our role in this learning is drawing attention to the specifics of emotional life—noticing and naming details and experiences. So, for example, when we're reading books with children, even their beginning books with few words, we can introduce the language of feelings—words like thrilled, gloomy, satisfied, or envious—as we talk about characters in the context of story events.

❧ *"In the story, it says 'the cows were growing impatient with the farmer.' Sometimes I feel impatient when I am waiting for everyone to finish cleaning up and I wish they would hurry up. Has anyone here felt impatient? What does impatient mean? [Clarifying as necessary.] Say the word impatient to your partner... Tell your partner about a time you felt impatient. Say, 'I was impatient when...'"*[4]
In this example, the teacher draws attention to the word in an authentic context, and provides a personal example of the emotion to which the children can relate. She then invites some children to offer examples from their own lives and to articulate the meaning of the word, explaining and clarifying as necessary. Next, she invites the children to articulate their own examples to each other, repeating the word as they go. Each time the children say the word, it builds a memory trace. To reinforce the concept, she might ask on another occasion, "What makes your parents impatient?" or "I'm feeling a little impatient. Can anyone say why?" or "Are you feeling a little impatient, Alex?" Using the word in multiple contexts expands the connections, the memory, and the meaning. We can think of this as simply vocabulary development, but it's also normalizing conversations about emotions, building understanding of how we and others feel—feelings that explain why we and others act as we do.

❧ *"Don't lean back in your chair like that because I care too much to see you get hurt."*[5]
Who hasn't had to correct a child for inappropriate behavior? Jeralyn Johnson's comment to one of her fourth graders corrects the errant behavior, but softens the correction by articulating the emotional-relational logic of her request. Without the caring part of the sentence, it would simply be a command, asserting a dominant relationship. Instead, her comment simultaneously normalizes the

expression of feelings and provides a caring foundation for class-room life. When students feel teachers care about them, they're more engaged and successful in school.[6]

🌱 *"I get nervous in front of a large group."*[7]

Merry Komar's comment to her second and third-grade class occurred when Aisha, a second-grade student in special education, balked at giving a book talk and began behaving problematically. Aisha had specifically asked to give the book talk. Her first. Imagining the cause of the behavior, Merry confessed that she, too, gets nervous about public speaking. Her students protested that was crazy because Merry was publicly speaking every day with them. So, she clarified: "I get nervous when I speak in front of a lot of *adults* I don't know. So, I go into the bathroom and do the Superman pose in front of the mirror and pretend I am Superwoman. Then I remember what I looked like when I get started talking. When I did that, I felt confident."

Merry's confession made Aisha's feelings of anxiety normal. Classmates went further, offering their own stories of anxiety. However, their stories, like Merry's, did not portray them as victims of anxiety. Rather, they asserted agency. Ellie reported that her anxiety about dance recitals was eased when her parents suggested she should imagine people in their underwear. Her strategy drew peals of laughter. Colin offered that he imagines that only his family is in the audience. With the anxiety monster defanged, Aisha was able to talk about her anxiety, noting that "I want to try something new but I don't want to embarrass myself." Merry pointed out that some people rehearse a talk with friends first, or write down their talk and read it, prompting offers from several classmates to be her rehearsal friend. This might have gone quite differently if Merry had viewed Aisha's actions as simply a behavior problem which her status as a special education student might easily have led to.

Normalizing conversations about feelings is important, but perhaps more importantly, Merry helps the children see how they can assert agency over their emotional lives, strategically anticipating and managing their emotions. As a resource, the class preserved the strategies on an interactive anchor chart, and the comment, "Aisha, look at how you helped all of us today," reestablished Aisha's position as a competent, contributing community member.

Emotional and behavioral management strategies like these can improve children's self-regulation. For example, you might recall Walter Mischel's studies in which young children sitting alone in a room with a marshmallow were offered the choice to eat it immediately or wait for the return of the experimenter, in which case they would instead get two marshmallows. When children are offered distancing strategies, such as imagining the marshmallows as clouds, or pretending the marshmallows are just a picture by mentally putting a frame around them, they become much better at waiting.[8] But self-regulation, as Merry approaches it, is not simply a skill. It's embedded in narratives that reflect a growth mindset. Such narratives move beyond teaching skills. For example, young children who heard a story in which a character struggled with waiting but ultimately experienced it as energizing ("the longer you wait, the stronger you feel"), became better at delaying gratification, actually *generating* strategies themselves.[9]

Children's ability to regulate their behaviors and emotions predicts their achievement test scores over and above socioeconomic status (SES) and intelligence, and across cultures.[10] Self-regulation predicts changes in report card grades even more strongly.[11] Young children with better self-regulation do better in math and literacy in the early grades, they have better social skills, and better health.[12] When they grow up, regardless of SES and childhood IQ, they're more successful, less likely to run afoul of the law, and continue to have better health.[13]

As adults, we daily encounter unbidden events that invite sometimes unwelcome emotional reactions—"trigger" words, or experiences we can't avoid, or even, like Aisha, events we initiate without anticipating our emotional reaction. Daily, we have to manage our responses to apparently thoughtless behaviors of colleagues, family members, or neighbors. Doctors, nurses, and emergency response personnel confront illness, injury, and death but, for their own sake and for the sake of others, they must manage their emotions and continue performing their duties. Though it's not always possible, we all try to find productive ways to manage and express our emotions so that we can live our best lives. Merry's conversations boost her students' emotional competence—and open brighter paths for their, and their friends' and families', futures.

❦ *"How does that feel?"*

This question opens conversations that help children recognize, articulate, and refine their understanding of their feelings. In connection with the associated event, it helps them think through the emotional implications of activities and incidents. It can be used when helping children understand social problems, by helping them articulate their feelings to each other. For example, "When he wouldn't let you have a turn on the computer, how did that make you feel?" The more children are able to accurately identify and articulate their feelings, the more their emotional and relational competencies develop, and the more they are able to imagine how others feel.

❦ *"How does that feel to finish your first non-fiction book?"*

An expansion of the previous question, this one also establishes the child as a bona fide author, opening the possibility of a new element of identity. It opens an agentive narrative—you made this book—while drawing attention to the associated positive feelings, increasing the likelihood of future book making. It also attaches an internal motivation to the act of book making. Rehearsing that connection is almost as good as the original experience and strengthens the positive motivational link. Building positive associations with valued activities is important. When kindergartner Alejandra helped her peer learn a new skill, Susie, her teacher, pointed out to her that her partner was actually using the skill.[14] She added, "Aren't you happy for your partner?" Catching her later, Susie prompted, "Did you help your partner?" The connection drew a big smile and a nod. To make the otherwise fleeting positive association a bit more permanent and conscious, it doesn't hurt to add, "How does that feel?"

❦ *"How do you think he felt about that, as a scientist?"*[15]

First-grade teacher Pegeen Jensen asks this sort of question about a book character, Snowflake Bently. Each of us is a complex of identities and children need to understand how those identities influence their emotions. As a father a person might have one set of feelings but as a scientist or a friend, quite another. These facets of identity routinely produce conflicts in our decisions and what we value. I, for example, am a father, husband, friend, researcher, gardener, writer, soccer player, and so forth. Each of these facets of my identity has a slightly different perspective in different situations. On Mothers' Day, do I go and play soccer, work on the chapter I'm trying to finish, help a friend move house, or do I spend the day pampering my wife? We are constantly trying to maintain a coherent self, while weaving these facets into a coherent whole. We can lean on identities to help children think through things. We can ask, for example, "As his friend, how are you thinking about that?"

❦ *"What would you be feeling right now if you were [the book character]?"*

It isn't just that children need to understand their own emotional lives; their social lives depend on them accurately understanding the emotional lives of others. When eighth-grade teacher Ms. Tucker asked the above question, she wasn't looking for a single answer, or even an answer directed to her. Rather she was simply provoking her students to imagine themselves into another's head—to expand their understanding of social and emotional life. Provocations like this increase students' engagement in their reading, and their engagement with the characters in narrative texts, which expands their empathy, just as it does for adults.[16]

The more general, "How do you think she feels about that?" comes up both in discussions of narrative fiction and in the daily management of classroom life. During classroom altercations, we ask how the participants in the dispute feel. We insist that students imagine themselves into the other's shoes, taking responsibility for the impact of their own actions on others—again, a central piece of agency and of democratic living. At the same time, we are building the mind reading necessary for children not only to comprehend the stories they read, but also to imagine the effect of their writing on audiences and to imagine why authors do what they do, enabling critical readings of others' writing.

Not all such provocations are equally powerful though. For example, "Imagine how you would feel if that happened to you" is more likely to increase prosocial behavior than is "Imagine how Emily feels." The former increases both empathic concern and the overlap between self and other. We can also increase this overlap with provocations like: "I can see why you would feel angry when he took your toy. I wonder how he felt when you were playing with toys and he didn't have one."

Developing children's mind reading in this way also allows them to see that stories are told from a perspective and other perspectives are not equally represented. A teacher might say, for example, "You know who I would like to hear from? I want to hear what [secondary book character] is feeling." Inviting children to collaboratively retell stories through different characters and inviting them to tell how they feel and what they think at particular points in their telling is another way of expanding this maturity. But emotions and thoughts are tangled up in complex ways. For example, when one of Ms. Tucker's eighth-grade students asserted that it wasn't logical for a book character to feel guilty for a sibling's death, Ms. Tucker asked "Doesn't grief cause you to think in irrational ways?" Untangling these connections among feelings, relationships, and contexts is an important element of emotional maturity. For example, we need to recognize how, when we are angry, our thoughts go in directions we might reconsider when the anger has passed.

There are complex and little understood relationships among these aspects of development. For example, children's mind reading is associated with their sense of well-being.[17] Stories told by children aged three to eight who have a solid sense of well-being contain more empathy and affiliation than do stories told by children with a weaker sense of well-being. These benefits are not picked up on state tests and the causal relationships remain unclear. However, if there is a chance that there are such side-benefits to be had—at no obvious cost—I say let's go for it. Understanding ourselves entails understanding others and how we are alike and not alike, seeing others in ourselves and ourselves in others. In the long run, the more we are able to orchestrate interactions in ways that allow us to think beyond ourselves and through each other, the more we evolve as a society and as individual human beings.

❧ *"[With your faces] show me 'fascinated.'"*

Jeralyn Johnson said this after encountering the word "fascinated" in a book she was sharing with her fourth graders. When her students contemplate how to respond, they must attend carefully to the details of the emotion and its expression. They might find a relevant experience to invoke the feeling, while being conscious of the nature of their physical expression. Why is this important? For mind reading to be an asset, it has to be fairly accurate. For that to happen, people need to accurately make sense of each other's emotional displays—their facial and bodily expressions as well as their verbal ones.

Jeralyn also approaches this problem from the other direction: "When I picked up this book, I made this face. What was I thinking?" Notice that, here, Jeralyn is inviting imagination, not only of feelings, but also of associated thoughts. Understanding thoughts as well as feelings requires bringing to bear the immediate expression, along with experience of the person's past behavior, which Jeralyn's students do when one answers, "You're going to push [challenge] us," and another says, "Sneaky." Social life requires recognizing others' emotions as part of effective communication.

So teachers ask, "What are you thinking?" and "What is she thinking?" as well as "How do you think she feels about that?" Inviting such conversations summons the use of mental verbs (imagine, feel, believe, wonder, want, like, etc.) and mental state language (sad, confused, enthusiastic, contrite, etc.), the use of which accelerates children's development. We are social animals, and the ability to imagine and reason about other's thoughts, actions, intentions, feelings, and beliefs is fundamental to social life. Social development is the foundation for intellectual and even physical health into adulthood. Well-developed mind reading enables understanding things from multiple perspectives, a foundation not just for positive social relationships but for the functioning of civil society. In blunt academic terms, it directly affects the child's ability to comprehend complex narratives, to argue more persuasively, and at least in five- to seven-year-olds, to better understand idiomatic expressions.[18] It's a foundation for critical literacy which requires adopting multiple perspectives, imagining others' intentions, and imagining social arrangements that might not yet exist.

The more children (and adults) are able to clearly articulate their feelings, the less others will need to imagine them and make mistakes. These conversations likely reduce the future breakdown of peer relationships, parent–child relationships, parent–parent relationships, and business relationships. They also likely reduce the problem of loneliness, and ultimately the need for mental health counseling. Plus, as we learned in Chapter 5, the more students find others' thoughts and feelings interesting, the more they are likely to hold a growth mindset.

🌱 *"Who else would like that book?"*

To respond sensibly to such a request, one must understand others' interests and capabilities. The unspoken assumption is that it's normal to talk with others about their books and their interests. At the same time, knowing more about one another in these ways makes it harder to be mean to one another. In classrooms that encourage this shared knowledge, children appear able to figure into their book suggestions both interest and level of competence without using relative competence as a bludgeon. Beyond that, as one student pointed out when asked who else would like the book, "Probably Patrick... He's, he's not the kind of guy who laughs, and he doesn't smile too much. And in this book, he might smile."[19]

Reading and writing, it turns out, are natural places to learn about others and some teachers actively use them for this purpose. Early in the school year June Williamson explained to her students, "We're doing biographies at the beginning of the year partially because it goes with what we're doing—getting to know each other and getting to know ourselves a little better."[20] Discussions of books similarly can lead to greater shared understanding, affiliation, and a sense of caring.[21]

🌱 *"You know what I heard you doing just now Claude? Putting yourself in her place. You may not have realized it. You said 'Will she ever shut up?' Which is what Zinny [book character] is thinking..."*[22]

This comment draws to the consciousness of the student and the class, a productive cognitive strategy that would otherwise have slipped by unnoticed. When they are engaged, children, and adults, often accomplish things without any awareness of what they have done. Automatic, fluent performance like this is a very efficient use of mental resources because it doesn't use up our limited conscious space. The downside is that when we encounter problems to which we do not respond so automatically, we can't recall those previous strategic options for the new situation. This comment to Claude makes the hidden mental skill of the individual into a future resource for both the individual and the community.

The comment actually does a couple of other useful things. It points out (implicitly) to Claude that what he did was a sensible thing to do, as a reader, and offers him the chance to claim competence and agency. It also opens the possibility of discussing the story from Zinny's point of view, noticing that stories are always presented from a point of view, and that some points of view are not given as much prominence as others. In other words, it opens a central conversation for critical literacy.

One of the important things we can do as teachers is spend more time getting to know students' perspectives and trying to empathize more with their feelings, particularly those of students who are different from us (whoever they and we are). When we think about empathizing, we tend to dwell on the experience of negative emotions. However, in a year-long study of a large sample of white teachers, Todd Pittinsky and Matthew Montoya found that teachers' empathic experience of the positive, joyful experiences of their students of color led to more positive feelings toward them, which led to more positive and proactive interactions with them and thus better academic outcomes.[23] After all, our language is emotionally loaded, and our pleasure in teaching tends to be infectious.[24] And positive emotions affect children's problem-solving and self-regulation, their social behavior, attachments, achievement, and relationship to school.[25] Even when happiness is below conscious awareness, it decreases the tendency to stereotype.[26] Negative emotions, particularly sadness, have the reverse effect. There's a lot to be said for arranging for students to experience joyful engagement in the classroom, and experiencing it with them.

Extension

Explain the significance of the following example of teacher talk for children's social, emotional, and academic development:

Did you notice the look on Poppa's face on this page when the tire goes flat? Look at his eyes and mouth. He looks like, "Oh no!" in that picture doesn't he? I think it's so neat the way Jill Barton showed on his face how he was feeling when his tire went flat. She must have really thought about what he would look like if that happened.[27]

Knowing

At its deepest reaches, education gave me an identity as a knower. It answered the question "Who am I?" [but it also answered the question] "what is the world?"... and the same knowledge that gave me a picture of myself and the world also defined the relation of the two... What is the nature of the knower? What is the nature of the known? And what is the nature of the relations between the two? These questions belong to a discipline called *epistemology*.

Parker Palmer[1]

The underlying epistemology of classroom interaction defines the bottom line for learning: what ultimately counts is *the extent to which instruction requires students to think, not just report someone else's thinking*.

Martin Nystrand and colleagues[2]

In most classrooms, teachers ask a lot of questions, the vast majority of which have a single expected answer (obviously not your classroom, dear reader, but humor me). In a British sample in the early grades, student responses lasted five seconds or less on average, and 70 percent of answers consisted of three words or less.[3] Only 10 percent of teacher questions were open and 15 percent of teachers asked no open questions. The common pattern of interaction between teachers and their students has been called the IRE for teacher Initiates, student Responds, and teacher Evaluates,[4] or sometimes IRF (for Feedback).[5] For example, consider the following interaction (T = teacher, S = student):[6]

T: We have been working all year on what is called sequence. What does sequence mean?   [Initiate]

S: Order?   [Respond]

T: That's right. [Evaluate] …Tell me some things that happened in *Mr. Popper's Penguins* and we'll put them in sequence. [Initiate]

S: He paints.   [Respond]

T: OK. That's one event…   [Evaluate]

S: The guy was walking on the roof.   [Respond]

T: OK, [Evaluate] do we know who? Does it give his name? [Initiate]

Ss: No. He's the tightrope walker.   [Respond]

T: Thank you James…   [Evaluate]

S: Captain Cook built a nest.   [Respond]

T: OK. Very good. [Evaluate] What is it called when a penguin builds a nest?   [Initiate]

This sequence is very controlling for a couple of reasons. First, the underlying premise is that the teacher already knows what needs to be known and therefore takes the role of judging the quality of the student's response, positioning the teacher in the role of authority and knowledge giver and the student as the knowledge receiver without authority. Second, the IRE might better have been called a QRE since the initiating language is almost always a question. Questions exert even more control by not only insisting on a response, but also by specifying the topic of the conversation, and often the form of the response. Questions that have, or suggest, right/wrong answers are even more controlling. The IRE offers an implicit answer to the questions posed above by Parker Palmer: Knowledge is composed of facts possessed by teachers, who have the authority to transmit them to children, and children only know about the world through the knowledge that is transmitted to them.

Classroom interaction based on the IRE is problematic not because it's inefficient, because as Robin Alexander points out, "by its own lights it can be very efficient… [but] because its account of efficiency is predicated on teaching as transmitting, learning as receiving and knowing as repeating."[7] It's also problematic as a primary interaction pattern because it creates cultural conflicts for students from a range of non-dominant cultures.[8]

There are alternatives to the IRE that are more culturally permeable, and in which children play a more active role in the ownership and construction of knowledge. As Barbara Rogoff and Chikako Toma point out:

> Learning to act as a recipient of information and to display receipt of the information... [is not the same as] building on ideas in a shared endeavor [in which] participants' roles can vary widely, such as leading a shared inquiry, playing around with an idea together, or closely following other people's lines of thought.[9]

The following examples of teacher talk lead to conversations the (unspoken) premise of which is that the students are thinkers with something to say that is worth listening to. These conversational pivots are, I believe, invitations to a more productive epistemology and are more culturally permeable.[10]

❧ *"What are you thinking?"*

This is an open request to contribute unfinished, rough draft thoughts. It's wide open, giving students lots of ways to contribute, and it implies that offerings won't be judged. It's an invitation to be heard, and the feeling that one is being heard matters, perhaps more than the content of what is being said.[11] If followed by something like, "Say more about that," or "Keep going with that idea," it shows students they are being heard and taken seriously, that they have something important to contribute to the intellectual community, while offering them a sense of belonging. The more we actually listen to students, the more they feel understood, cared for, and that their contributions to the community are valued, all of which are linked to greater engagement, achievement, self-esteem, and overall well-being.[12]

Merry Komar takes notes of what her second and third-grade students say during book discussions, not only to reflect on the changing qualities of conversations, and to take stock of learning, but also because she can later directly quote particular students, showing them how important their voices are. Also, incidentally, it keeps her from constantly intruding on the conversation.

❧ *"Let's see if I've got this right" [then summarizes student's extended comments].*

This move establishes a new base from which to see how far we've come and upon which to build further thinking if that seems warranted. By reflecting to the students their comments, the teacher at once validates their voice, shows she is listening, and opens the possibility for students to reflect on, modify, or challenge what has been said. Unless intonation says otherwise, this takes the evaluation aspect out of the teacher's role. Another version would be, "Let's hold up for a moment and see where we are." While accomplishing the same thing, this version casts the teacher not so much as a listening other, but as a community member helping the community strategically manage its inquiry process. It does this by shifting from *I* to *we*. It can also be helpful to follow up with "Did I get that right?" to invite correction or modification of the summary. Doing so again positions the teacher as supporting the children's thinking, and the children as the agents of knowledge production.

❦ *"Any questions? Let's start with these." [Teacher writes them on a chart].*
The effect of soliciting *students'* questions is to cede control of the topic of conversation to the students, or at least to engage in more balanced negotiation of the topic—provided the questions are taken seriously and followed up on. The questions then become matters of inquiry, which have further important properties.[13] Among other things, they suggest a very different role for the student in the production of knowledge. They also change the students' conception of what school is about and its relation to their own personal interests. When students have listed a substantial number of questions, they can then decide which ones are the most important to pursue. The result is that they become increasingly good at asking interesting questions, particularly if they are encouraged to analyze their questions.[14] For example, one teacher names a particular kind of question, "So, if you asked those questions of anyone in the class, they would have something to say on that. They're big questions." The ability or tendency to ask effective questions contributes a great deal to children's agency, and to their development of critical literacy.

This is not as easy as it sounds. Because of the epistemologies in which most of us were schooled, many of us, as teachers, feel compelled to answer students' questions when we know the answers—which we feel we should. Indeed, if we don't answer them, sometimes the students are outraged by our violation of what they thought was a pretty clear contract. Consequently, they might initially insist that their teacher take up the monologic position of sole authority. They know how school is supposed to be done, and staying within the familiar role, even if oppressive, is easier.

❦ *"[Silence]."*

Sometimes called "wait time," the attentive silence following a child's comment might better be called "thinking time." In most classrooms teachers do most of the talking, and children's thinking time is minimal.[15] However, teachers' wait times are unevenly distributed. They offer more thinking time for more successful students than for less successful students.[16]

On the face of it, remaining silent seems quite trivial, but extending thinking times is positively related to more student talk, more sustained talk, and more "higher order" thinking.[17] Indeed, sometimes teachers deliberately slow conversation down and foreground the "thinking" part in order to develop more reflective habits. For example, when her students had arrived at a solution to a problem, Joan Backer asked them how they could check and then said, "Just digest that question for a minute... [long pause]."[18] In a similar way, she might say, "This is a complicated question, so let's take some time to just think about it."

When a teacher waits, she is offering the floor to the students. In a one-to-one conference it can be the same as saying, "Can you say more about that?" a phrase that such teachers also use. The overall message is something like "I'm interested in what you have to say," which positions the child as having authority. This invites identity development that includes "I am a person whose experience and knowledge matter." Thinking time also offers respect—a relational property that is the life-blood of a learning community. When teachers wait for a child to figure something out or self-correct, it conveys the message that they expect the child is capable of doing it. Failure to wait conveys the opposite message.

❦ *"I wonder..."*

This represents a class of linguistic lubricants. It marks the offering of a possible hypothesis, or a tentative idea with an invitation, but not an insistence, for others to pick it up and improve it or take it further. Teachers can use these uncertainty markers in order to participate in a class discussion while minimizing their positional power, making it possible for students to analyze and possibly critique the teacher's contribution. Other "tentativeness markers"[19] include: "maybe," "seems like," "perhaps," "or something," "I think," and so forth. These markers also enable more expansive group discussions too, what Neil Mercer calls "exploratory talk,"[20] talk that brings multiple minds together to explore a problem in the most powerful ways, which we'll return to in the next chapter.

🌱 *"I hadn't noticed that until Antoine pointed it out."*[21]
This comment levels the power difference between teacher and students making space for student agency in the knowledge-building practices of the classroom. It establishes the child's status and identity as an agentive knowledge contributor, increasing the likelihood of his, and others', continued active engagement. In a book discussion, Merry Komar responded to one of her students' noticings with, "I didn't notice that." Later in the conversation another student commented, "When I first read it, I didn't notice it, but then when Tom said that, I noticed it." These exchanges are basically saying, "I learned from you," acknowledging the other's contribution to the community and thus recognizing their competence. I suspect they also contain an element of gratitude. Such comments also show the children that they are being heard, which, as I noted earlier, has important benefits.

🌱 *"That's a very interesting way of looking at it. I hadn't thought about it that way. I'll have to think about it some more."*[22]
I need to give some context for the significance of this comment. The class was discussing a book early in the year, and a student from a marginalized ethnic group made a comment that, from a dominant cultural perspective, made no obvious sense. His teacher looked thoughtful and then said, "That's a very interesting way of looking at it. I hadn't thought about it that way. I'll have to think about it some more." The epistemological view communicated to the student is, "I don't expect everyone to think about this in the same way. I respect you and what you have to say. Keep offering possibilities because I expect to learn from them." It asserts that the teacher does not have all the answers, that perspectives are bound to vary, that stretching to understand different perspectives is expected

and valued, and that students (including ones whose perspectives are different from that of the teacher) have important things to say.

In the most practical terms, the comment acts to keep the student in the conversation. Failure to accomplish this would make the teacher's job, with that student, very difficult indeed. It's comments like this one in situations that would make many teachers uncomfortable, that reveal real teaching competence, particularly because the teacher is not faking it. She genuinely believes she might learn from the student.

❧ *"I don't know, but how could we find out?"*

Mary Cowhey, a first- and second-grade teacher, reported: "Time and again, when children ask me good questions, I must say, "I don't know, but how could we find out?"[23] Mary's question makes it clear that she is not the source of all knowledge, offering neither the knowledge sought, nor a strategy for gaining it, both of which could be dependency-producing. Rather, she positions the two of them as joint knowledge-seekers (we), and invites the child to take control of the knowledge-building process. Her prompt is conditional (how *could* we)—she isn't insisting that the child find an answer, which might take the thrill out of it, and her prompt is open to more than one possible solution. Mary would likely provide some assistance along the way, but would keep the child in control of the inquiry. Over time (time and again) Mary's response builds a connection for the children—I have a question: How could I find an answer? One of her students at the end of the year wrote to her: "Thank you for teaching us what you knew and what you didn't." She took that as a compliment.

❧ *"How did you know?"*

This question follows a pupil's assertion of some knowledge— a word spelling, a fact, or a solution. It invites a narrative about the production of knowledge, checking warrants (sources of evidence or authority), and theorizing. Whether or not the attempt was correct, the question assumes it was an intelligent effort. In this way it's similar to asking "How would someone arrive at that answer [position, etc.]?" It assumes a knowledgeable, thinking person, even though, on this occasion, they might not have been quite correct or successful. It's this assumption of a knowledgeable and agentive person that is the important message—the more powerful because it's not overtly stated and therefore not open to contestation. The question also turns the emphasis toward *knowing* rather than *knowledge*. Taking seriously how people know what they presume to know is an important aspect of critical literacy. Along these same lines, there are questions like: "Can you give an example?" or "Remember to give evidence in support of your perspective."

❦ *"How could we check?"*

This question, a close relative of the previous one, can appear at the level of figuring out a word while reading or writing, or examining a hypothesis or theory in science, social studies, literature, or examining political statements. The productive epistemology represented by this family of questions and comments (such as, "How could we be sure?" "What makes you think that?") is one that places children in agentive roles with respect to knowledge production, with all of the rights and responsibilities that confers.

The responsibility means that children must cross-check their sources and warrants. They begin to ask themselves these questions and expect to ask them with and of others. They require the student to use sources of information or logic to boost confidence in their construction of knowledge rather than having to seek verification from an outside authority. In some of these comments, the teacher has used the word "we" ("How could we check?") to move the burden of justification to the group rather than the individual. This prevents the individual offering the knowledge from being publicly unable to accomplish the task, while including them in the invitation to do so. As students offer possibilities and the group collectively thinks through the problem, the individual can acquire the thinking process of the group, a point I will explore more fully in the next chapter.

❦ *"Is that an observation or conjecture?"*[24]

This question came during a week in which science, and various other aspects of class life, revolved around the birth of ducklings in the classroom. Children were routinely taking turns observing and documenting the behavior and development of the ducklings. The question asks the students to distinguish between observation and inference, to attend to the relationship between warrants and claims. It also points out to them the human tendency to add extra layers of meaning to observation. As Deanna Kuhn and her colleagues observe, "By the end of the first year of life, infants have begun to make causal inferences based on the juxtaposition of an antecedent and an outcome... it is the fact that this inference strategy is overlearned that causes problems."[25] The question also asks students to attend to their (and others') use of language. These are central aspects of critical literacy.

❧ *"Thanks for straightening me out."*[26]

This teacher comment to a student implies something about the power differential between them and the epistemology in operation. The comment implies that a student has done what in most classes would be unthinkable—evaluated the teacher's comments. This teacher's response, however, tells the child that, not only is it acceptable in this classroom, but helping others correct misconceptions is something to be encouraged. The response at once asserts the authority of the child in the discourse, the fallibility of the teacher, and that both are *engaged in the same intellectual project* so that preventing miscommunications and correcting errors are joint concerns. This joint intellectual adventure is the central concept of a community of inquiry. Another teacher made this clear in her response to a student's question, "I really don't know. I have no idea. Let's find out because... you know what, I'm interested to find out myself."[27] For many of us, it's hard to say this to the students, that we don't have the answer; however, this response is powerful. It reasserts the common (*let's*) intellectual project, positioning the student in an active role, and strengthens the motive for researching the question particularly by affirming its significance. At the same time as increasing the likelihood of the student asking more questions, it opens the possibility of exploring "How can we research this question?"

Taking this line of thinking further, fourth-grade teacher June Williamson commented to her students, "*Never* believe everything I say. Never believe everything *any* adult says. I might say five is prime, but can you prove it?"[28] Her comment confirms that *nobody* has a corner on truth and that authority should always be questioned, checked, and warrants sought. This is another central component of the critical literacy aspect of epistemology. It naturalizes human fallibility and asserts that no authority is above error, no matter how well intentioned or authoritatively positioned. More than that, though, children in such classrooms are not forced into the epistemic role of merely remembering the knowledge that has been communicated to them by teachers and texts. They learn that language is not simply a vehicle for communicating information. Children in these classrooms do not deny the communicative function of language, but view the multiple sources of language in the classroom—teacher, books, internet, students, and their own language—as tools for thinking.[29]

I do not mean to imply here that these teachers never lecture or never engage in brief IRE sequences. The IRE has a place in classroom life in brief reviews or walking through a sequence of complex ideas.[30] However, when the bulk of classroom interactions take the IRE form, in which students are competing to give the correct answer, students come to believe that learning is primarily about being seen to be correct rather than about collaborative knowledge building.[31] Clear explicit telling certainly has its place too. In writing this book, I asked colleagues for commentaries on drafts, I sought and received the occasional mini-lecture or its print equivalent (reading books and articles). These instances of people "delivering information" did not interfere with my sense that I was inquiring into the meanings of what teachers say in classrooms, or eliminate my sense that I was working on an "improvable object."[32] There are so many things for me to understand if I am to advance my thinking about teaching. I will use all the help I can get. Just because I am inquiring does not mean that I have to learn everything from scratch. But finding productive ways to ask will become more important than current schooling practices suggest,[33] and the skill of my colleagues in deciding how much to tell and how to tell it should also not be underestimated. Learning these skills requires a community in which they are routinely practiced.

Extension

If you would like to shift the conversations in your classroom in the direction I have described, begin by planning ways to get children into open public conversations.

1 Analyze the following interaction from Debbie Miller's classroom.[34] Notice the ways in which she positions the students with respect to each other, herself, and the subject they are studying,

and how she extends their sense of agency. Consider any other comments you might add, or what you might do differently.

DM: Oh you guys, look at all this new learning. What's going on. Can you talk to me about what you've been doing?

S1: Well we learned a lot.

DM: Well tell me some of the things you've learned.

S1: Well I learned that the ocean has layers.

S2: Yeah.

DM: So what does that mean it has layers?

S1: Like, you know what in the rainforest has layers? Well it's just like it except in the rainforest it has more layers than… this only has three//… three.

S2: //yeah three.

DM: So you mean like in the ocean there's a top layer, is that how it goes? And then a middle layer…

S1: and a bottom layer.

DM: Wow.

S2: Yeah and I learned that the twilight layer… zone… is the is the middle layer.

DM: Yeah.

S2: It is 1,000 meters below.

DM: Below where?

S2: The surface.

DM: Oh the surface. Perfect.

[After further discussion]

DM: It's so interesting. I'm learning so much just sitting here. I better let you guys get back to work. Thank you for teaching me about those kinds of fish. And is the rest of your plan just to keep reading and recording?

S1: Yeah. You see this one?

DM: Keep going. You guys are doing great.

2 Next time you are reading aloud to the students, ask no questions and begin a pattern of annotating and pausing. At interesting points, say "Wow," and pause expectantly, or say, "I wonder if [some possibility]…" and pause. Most of all, if anyone says anything, show interest—"Oh, interesting…[with enthusiasm]"—then

pause. Under no circumstances offer any hint of judgment— "good," "right," "yes," etc. Offer a relevant comment, like, "I've felt like that before… [pause]." When you do ask questions, make them wide open, like, "Anyone else had that sort of feeling (experience)?" The rules of engagement for you include not judging any responses and providing ample thinking time. If pausing for longer than a breath is difficult for you, try counting slowly in your head to five—or ten—before picking up where you left off.

3 Get a conversation going in which you are not likely to be at the center. Marg Wells used the following strategy with second graders.[35] First, they conducted a survey in the class, asking their concerns about their lives in and out of school, about their neighborhoods and the world. In that context, they asked what made the children worried, angry, or happy, and what they would like to change. From this came topics that were relevant and engaging for the children and that brought multiple perspectives, and commitment.

4 Get the children to ask questions about a book you have read with them. Encourage as many as possible and write them on chart paper. Censor none. Read them all back commenting on what an interesting collection of questions they have, but since they obviously won't have time to find answers to all of them, perhaps they could select three to answer or think through either as a class or in small (diverse) groups with their own selections. Once they can do that, you can get a little fancy by getting them to ask questions addressed to the author—like what they would like to know that was not in the text.

5 With older students, if only some are prepared to engage with issues in book discussions for one reason or another, write a controversial position sentence on the board and see who agrees or disagrees. For example, having read *Puss in Boots*, the statement might be: "In this book, Puss lies to everyone and even murders someone all for his own benefit. He is not the 'good guy.'" If they are reluctant to take a position for whatever reason, ask them to go and stand by the position (yea or nay) by which they are most persuaded, understanding that as the class discusses the issue they can change their position. In science, they might do this with predictions and then discuss how they might establish credibility for their positions.

9 An Evolutionary, Democratic Learning Community

Democracy is neither a possession nor a guaranteed achievement. It is forever in the making; it might be thought of as a possibility—moral and imaginative possibility. For surely it has to do with the way persons attend to one another, care for one another, and interact with one another. It has to do with choices and alternatives, with the capacity to look at things as though they could be otherwise.

Maxine Greene[1]

Citizens in a democracy have the convictions and enthusiasms of their own responses, yet they are willing to keep an open mind about alternate points of view, and finally are able to negotiate meanings and actions that respect both individual diversity and community needs.

To overcome our tendency to follow authority blindly, we need to develop confidence in our own ability to interpret and judge what we observe around us in the world. But confident and out-spoken individuals must be complemented by a tradition of conduct for reconciling differences among their responses.

Gordon Pradl[2]

The foundation of humanity's evolutionary success is that we are biologically social—social to our genetic, cellular, and hormonal core.[3] Consequently, the qualities of our relationships affect our individual physical and mental well-being and development, and the qualities of the communities that sustain that development.[4] We are dependent on one another for our development. It's our mediation of this apparent weakness with cultural tools like language that turns it into our super power—our ability to collaborate and use distributed intelligence. In other words, the language we choose will profoundly affect the relational and emotional life of the classroom and the lives, development, and futures of its inhabitants.

Recall that "children grow into the intellectual life around them" and that the intellectual life is deeply social. The social relationships within which children learn are a part of their learning. Children, just like adults, learn better in a supportive environment in which they can risk trying out new strategies and concepts and stretching themselves intellectually. But learning communities are not simply about being supportive. For them to be evolutionary, they also require challenge from different perspectives, not as a contest for power, but to "help each other and check each other's tendencies to purely idiosyncratic or self-interested thinking."[5]

Some teachers are particularly good at building learning communities in which individuals feel valued and supported, and that sustain productive and critical learning. Children must have the experience of such communities if they are to know what they are aiming for in constructing their own learning environments. Students in British and American schools have limited histories in this regard. Even when they work in groups, they rarely work *as* a group, sharing ideas and working toward a common goal.[6] Since we tend to internalize the kinds of conversations in which we become involved, we should think seriously about the nature of these school interactions and their implications.

Children need to understand how to construct or become involved in learning communities so they can extend their own (and society's) development. The comments in this chapter show how teachers pull this off, teaching children to build caring and respectful learning communities, communities that are playful, but in which participants take each other's ideas seriously, exercising individual and collective agency in the process of getting things done. A basic property of such communities is that they have some shared understanding of the situation and activity they are jointly engaged in. This doesn't mean that they all agree, but they agree to try to understand each other in order to become mutually involved. They agree to be parts of the same social mind for a period of time.[7] For example, in such classrooms, they don't think they're engaged in a "read-aloud," they think they are engaged in "thinking together about a book." The former is something a teacher does while students listen. The latter demands collective participation, has implications for how children are positioned with respect to one another and the teacher, and requires addressing the ways children engage with one another.

To think together productively, participants need to share a set of principles of participation. If participants play a role in thinking through and generating and updating those principles, they will have less difficulty adhering to them. In my experience and in reported research, the principles people generate quite consistently include the need for listening to and respecting each other, ensuring that everyone's voice is heard, giving reasons for agreement or disagreement, and working toward agreement. Posting the principles a class develops and updating them as necessary will hasten the development of productive thinking together.

Listening to each other is central to collaborative learning communities. A friend once confessed to having missed an important piece of information in a conversation, blaming it on his need for a hearing aide. His wife assured him that his need was not for a hearing aide, but for a listening aide. Listening is a crucial part of learning from and with one another. Listening is harder when we think we are trying to win an argument in which we are certain we are right and the other person is wrong. It's easier when we find the topic personally relevant and meaningful. It's easier when we think it will serve our own interests, when we are confident that we might learn something interesting, or when it's key to our participation in a valued activity. That's why we help children notice the self-interested advantages of listening.

❦ *"Did you hear what Tim said? Stephen, would you repeat what he said for us so we can think about it?"*

In a discussion that had become a little noisy, Pegeen Jensen asked her first graders, "Did you hear what Tim said?" Then, foregrounding their careful listening to each other, asked Stephen to repeat Tim's comment. If instead she had asked Tim to repeat what he had said, or simply repeated it herself, her students would get the message that they did not need to listen to each other, just wait until the teacher arranged for them to hear the important stuff.

Listening carefully requires making sure that you understand the speaker, which means asking questions, when necessary, as Cheryl McMann pointed out to her fifth graders: "When you don't understand what someone said, remember, it's your job to ask them to explain."[8] Her relational observation insists on listeners' agency and responsibility—a responsibility because, as I pointed out earlier, feeling heard really matters.[9] It has a similar effect to an act of kindness.

❦ *"What are you thinking? Stop and talk to your neighbor about it."*

This instruction, in the middle of a read-aloud, draws children's attention to their intellectual processes, building metacognitive awareness, and in the process develops the capacity to share, and thus expand, those processes. It's an open question to which everyone can respond. And talking to a neighbor rather than the whole group allows all the children to have a voice, which would be more time-consuming with the whole group. At the same time, it helps children to understand that meaning-making is not a matter of getting the right answer since they quickly learn how different people make different, yet similar, sense. In addition, the more they get to have such personal conversations with their classmates, the more they know them and the less they are able to view them through stereotypes or to put them down. Stereotype and domination are made possible by the reduction of the complexity of others to the handful of features that mark them as different—as not-me.

❦ *"So, Melinda, you really listened to Anthony's idea, and the two of you stayed focused on it and talked more about it. Now you both understand something about this text and what the author is doing that you didn't understand before."*[10]

This comment came from fourth-grade teacher Don Reed after he restarted two students whose conversation had broken down. He helped them see that careful listening led to an interesting conversation and new learning for each of them. Without his comment, the causal relationship between listening, conversation, and learning—a self-interest motive, and an agentive strategy—would likely have slipped by unnoticed. If we expect children to do these things, we need to help them see what's in it for them. So, it's worth highlighting how students' interesting thoughts and contributions are often provoked by listening to others.

❦ *"I notice, Laurel, that when he was talking it sort of jogged your mind—what were you thinking?"*[11]

This observation-question has the same leaning as the previous comment because it also turns children's attention to the significance of group processes. Rather than inviting a narrative of joint agency, it tells one. It's the same conversation but from a different classroom. It occurred during a discussion in which the teacher was playing primarily a monitoring role. One child had the floor and was clarifying a point when a second, Laurel, said, "Oh. Oh." and raised her hand to speak. In inviting her to speak, the teacher pointed out to her (and the assembled group) the significance of others' ideas for one's own thinking.

This, again, offers a self-interested motive for listening closely to others, and also a motive for appreciating others. There was evidence in this class that the students did indeed become aware of this. I recorded examples of children taking extra time and effort to try to understand unusual comments by peers—observations that would have been ignored or scorned in many classrooms. These interactions suggested to me that, consistent with their teacher's invitation, the children had come to value different perspectives as a resource for their own thinking and learning. Children need to learn tolerance, but as a foundation for social relationships, the understanding that difference is in your own best interests beats "tolerance" hands-down. Tolerance is about resisting a tendency to judge difference negatively, and is often simply a part of indifference. By contrast, this classroom conversation assumes difference to be a valuable resource for individuals.

Notice that a planned lesson on this would likely be less effective than capitalizing on the concrete event as it happened. However, some comments, like the following, explicitly insist on this understanding and can be pre-planned: "Make sure each person has a chance to say something so that you're sure you don't miss different ways of thinking about it." This comment provides the self-interested frame for ensuring all voices are heard. Having different perspectives in your head allows you to monitor and self-check your own thinking. Having multiple perspectives on the table provokes deeper thinking in order to resolve the uncertainties they produce.

To take this further, we also encourage children to notice when certain voices are missing from the conversation, and help them see how bringing them into the conversation will be individually and collectively beneficial. During a second- and third-grade book discussion group, a group member, Claire, invited into the conversation Shauna, a quiet student who often missed classroom discussions to go down the hall to her special education class—a practice that can make such students feel like outsiders in their own class. An excellent discussion ensued. Teacher Kathy Champeau drew the students' attention to their enjoyment of the discussion then asked: "If Claire hadn't invited Shauna into the conversation, what would have happened?"[12] Her question requires the students to construct the causal relationship between inviting in the quiet student and the quality of the ensuing experience.

It's worth considering what led to Claire inviting Shauna into the conversation. Kathy had noticed that Shauna looked as though she had something to say but had not been able to get into the conversation. Kathy asked the group whether they noticed anything about Shauna and Claire said that she thought Shauna had something to say but hadn't been able to say it. So Kathy asked whether anyone else had had that experience and what it felt like—expanding their empathic concern for Shauna. Moving from empathy to action, Kathy commented: "So when we see this happening, when people aren't able to get their thinking into the conversation, we have to invite them in." Keeping the ball in Claire's court, she added, "So why don't you invite her into the conversation, Claire?"[13] Notice that Kathy didn't invite Shauna in herself. At every step of the way she kept Claire as the person with agency. This process provided two motives for inviting diversity into the conversation—empathy, and self-interest. Following the successful event, she could privately ask Claire how that felt to have helped Shauna and thus contributed to the learning community.

During a different book discussion in the same class, a more vociferous student invited one of the quieter students into the conversation. At the end of the conversation, another student observed: "It was a good thing we asked Yacoub to speak because he had something important to say." Students' talk is very much influenced by the talk in which they are immersed. And actually, once a dialogic culture has been established, the number of words individual children speak is unrelated to their achievement because quiet students are still actively participating even if not always out loud.[14]

🌱 *"So, we have two different points of view. We're thinking [summarizes perspective 1] or maybe [summarizes perspective 2]. What do the rest of you think?"*[15]

Cheryl summarized for her fifth graders two perspectives that have arisen in the book discussion, normalizing the multiplicity of perspectives and inviting dialogue around the contrast. Notice, however, that she doesn't name the individuals who contributed the ideas. Rather, she says *"we're* thinking…" marking the ideas as part of their collective agency and responsibility in thinking together. When the ideas are separated from people they can be critiqued. And when that happens, people are more creative, they generate more ideas, and they are more satisfied with the outcomes than when ideas are associated with particular people or when there is no criticism at all.[16] We might still identify children's contributions to the discussion but associating them with strategic acts like pushing back, building on, providing evidence or logic, inviting in a new voice, and so forth.

The use of "we" is also important for another reason. It presumes as the default that everyone in the group is a member of the learning community. "We" is an invitation to, and expression of, solidarity or affinity. Teachers using collective pronouns in their interactions encourage collective stories in the students. For example, asking, "Okay, so where are we in this?" invites the response, "We're…"

Of course, this is more likely to happen when there are community projects in which everyone, or at least groups of people, are collectively involved. Joint activity around shared goals produces not only the ability and desire to collaborate, but also a tacit understanding that doing so is normal. Connecting children's feelings to effective group processes along the way helps ensure that they actually seek such processes, thus placing themselves in potential learning situations. So, for example, after students have had a highly engaging discussion, we might point out, "I notice that often happens when we disagree and listen carefully to each other." This is at the core of collaborative knowledge building and, not incidentally, democracy.

🌱 *"Would you agree with that?"*

On the occasion this question was offered, it invited public disagreement and the need to seek further information on a topic. It's a good way to set up the public need to articulate the logic of one's position. As one student articulates their logic, attempting to persuade others, and another strategically responds with their logic, the collective thinking becomes more complex and nuanced. Knowing how others think improves children's ability to imagine the intentions and logic of other social beings, something they will bring to their critical reading and their writing, if we encourage them to do so. The invitation to disagree indicates that disagreement is expected, indeed normal—a necessary understanding for thinking clearly and for participating in a democratic society.

Another version of this is "could someone play the devil's advocate?" The best way to check the quality of a theory or explanation is to have someone either critique it or make and defend an opposing theory. Over time, children need to become adept at doing this for themselves, or at least capable of non-defensively inviting others to take up the role. It's an ability that is essential for science, law, and other human endeavors for cross-checking. As students take different positions on an issue, they will push each other to articulate the logic of their position. In doing so, they make their thinking strategies available to others, who then take up those strategies. Once a student uses a strategy in the conversation, there is about a 90 percent chance it will be used again. With each use it's even more likely to be used again, more quickly than before and by more students.[17] In the process, students' skills at persuasion grow substantially and transfer to their writing.

🌱 *"Thanks Damon and Zelda. If you hadn't disagreed, we never would have got to the bottom of that."*

This comment implicitly emphasizes the collaborative nature of thinking together and the agency of individual community members. Consistent with research, it draws a causal connection between disagreement and improvement in the quality of the collective thinking.[18] You probably noticed the comment names two students. This might seem to fly in the face of not identifying students with particular ideas. However, this comment links students with a productive *strategy* rather than an idea. Foregrounding the collective benefit of strategically disagreeing can help override the disincentive of being the one whose idea didn't work out. We want disagreement and multiple perspectives to be seen as normal, and positive, something that often leads to deeper understanding. So we encourage children to disagree in the interests of clarifying and expanding thinking, and to recognize what difference brings into the conversation.

🌱 *"Are there any other ways to think about that? Any other opinions?"*

According to research, this sort of invitation does not happen often in school. Few classrooms in the United States entertain or encourage conflicting viewpoints.[19] We simply don't ask children to agree or disagree with each other or elaborate on each other's ideas in discussions—to use "other students' statements as thinking devices."[20] This is a great loss, because doing so has many benefits. First, it encourages students to seek and articulate warrants and logic for their preferred positions. This makes their thinking strategies available as part of the intellectual environment within which their individual and collective development occurs. Taking on the search for warrants and logic builds independence. Children who are used to this sort of invitation, and thus engage in dialogue, use words like "because," "if," and "why" more often than students who are not used to engaging in dialogue.[21] It turns out that thinking, as opposed to imitation, requires more than two possible perspectives, interpretations, universes, framings, or solutions.

Second, the conceptual conflicts likely to arise make it possible for children to change and expand their conceptual development. Cognitive change takes place when learners must confront and coordinate conflicting viewpoints and, as they resolve the conflicts, children participate in their own development.[22] Disagreement, more than agreement, moves children's thinking forward.[23] Third, in experiencing their own conceptual growth in such learning situations children start to learn that difference is beneficial to them personally, especially if we help them notice this as it's happening. This understanding is more powerful than the concept of tolerance. Tolerance requires a degree of maintenance since it's not obviously in the individual's self-interest.

Fourth, encouraging the engagement of multiple perspectives is a practice that is essentially demanded by a democratic society,[24] and therefore demanded in preparation for participation in a democratic society. Normalizing the concept that there are multiple possibilities, and that alternative perspectives frequently help us arrive at a better, more nuanced understanding of the focus of our inquiry, or a more elegant solution to a problem, is a big deal.

Another important function of inviting a range of perspectives is that it expands children's mind reading,[25] which, as we saw in Chapter 7, is central to many aspects of literate development. If you can't imagine an institutional perspective or a female perspective, or an Islamic perspective, then critical reading possibilities are limited. You can't imagine how something might have been written differently, how particular people's voices and perspectives are missing from a piece of writing. In the same way, you can't persuasively write to audiences whose perspectives you can't imagine. Neither can you convincingly construct such characters in fiction.

❦ *"Jaylen, your idea builds on Kiara's idea, now the idea is bigger."*

This comment recognizes Jaylen and Kiara as knowledge contributors and shows how together they can build more knowledge, bigger ideas, by adding on to each other's. We can emphasize this understanding by directly inviting students to contribute in that way: "Can anyone build on this idea?" Sometimes we also ask students to hold on to their new ideas while we "dig in" to, or "grow" an idea that's already on the table. We explain why and, later, return to recognize the thinking that was held in check, and the generosity and logic of doing so.

Language choices can make a big difference in whether discussions end in expanded understanding or relational catastrophe. We encourage children to provide their logic with their ideas, to notice when others don't, and to ask for it. We even show them how, by modeling, prompting, and perhaps by inviting them to think about what words they might use, and create an anchor chart. So we normalize language like: "Could you explain?" or "Why do you think that?" and "I agree, *because*," "I respectfully disagree, *because*," "I agree, and," or "I have evidence," or add qualifiers, like "sometimes..." What they can't do is make it personal, because that will lead to less productive, less creative conversations.

Once children have begun using constructive language, when discussions break down, we can remind them of what they are doing so they can bring to bear the skills they have developed. For example, Kathy Champeau reminded a group of second and third graders, "You know how to think together. What could you do next?"[26] When they successfully collaboratively accomplish something, we invite them to review the process that led to their success.

❧ *"You managed to figure that out with each other's help. How did you do that?"*

This is an invitation to tell a particular kind of narrative—a non-heroic one. In this story, there is a process (strategy or series of strategies) in which a problem is solved because people collaborated. Rehearsing the collaborative process positions students in relationships that make them admirable for different kinds of contribution, the nature of which can be reviewed by the teacher after the telling. This kind of narrative is the narrative of democratic living. It reminds children that often they cannot accomplish things by themselves and that collectively they can have more power than individually. For critical social action, this is very important learning. The children are learning how to use and manage the social and intellectual space they inhabit.

❧ *"How do you know when a conversation is finished?"*

This particular question came about when a book discussion group had deteriorated into something less than that, and somewhat disruptive. The teacher went over to the group and rather than reprimanding them, asked what the problem was, to which she received several simultaneous answers. She said, "It sounds as though you are having difficulty figuring out when a conversation is finished. How do you decide a conversation is finished?" She added that perhaps they could think through the process of their discussion group by audio-recording it the next day and doing some analysis. Fourth graders, mind you. It's this learning about how to manage not just one's own cognition, but the source of one's cognition in the learning environment that makes these conversations evolutionary. To over-simplify a tad, it's like learning how to manage not only the computer, but the computer networks for your own development. Since doing so requires understanding how to approach and manage difference not only in morally productive ways, but also in ways that are mutually sustaining, this sort of process is evolutionary in terms of democratic living.

🌱 *"This is how you go about making a large decision with a lot of parts. You take it in parts. Discussion is now open on how to decide which ones."*[27]
The fourth graders had just spent some time debating the ethics of dissecting duck eggs that were past gestation—a discussion that turned out to be a very complex moral dilemma parallel in complexity to the debates on abortion. However, the discussion had reached a point of no progress. Joan broke the decision down into a sequence of separate decisions on chart paper and explained the process, providing an example of explicit strategy instruction. The children, after brief discussion of each decision, were able to come to almost unanimous decisions on each. I have been in many meetings in which adults have been unfamiliar with this sort of social intellect management. Though such skills do not appear on any of the high-stakes tests, they are of considerable social and even economic value.

As adults, we must be able to use distributed thinking to overcome the limitations of our own experience and logic. We must learn to use the diversity of experience, perspective, and intellectual resources to solve the problems that arise in democratic living, but also to ratchet forward our own intellectual development. Children entering adulthood already apprenticed into these ways of knowing and being will certainly be sought after by both private- and public-sector employers. Peter Senge has described what he calls "learning organizations," arguing that not just individuals, but organizations must be set up to learn.[28] But, of course, the two are not independent.

More importantly, we live in a democracy, and strong democracy requires that we have a learning society.[29] As James Bovard puts it, "Democracy must be more than two wolves and a sheep voting on what to have for dinner."[30] It's not enough to vote, we must participate in collectively generating the most productive solutions to social problems, with the understanding that we will disagree, and that the disagreement can extend us to possibilities we could not have imagined. I am confident that before leaving elementary school, children from some classrooms have achieved this sense of agency and the *expectation* that they will be involved in such conversations. To the extent that they (and we) see education as not being about simply gaining more knowledge, but about increasing their ability to formulate and solve meaningful problems, we will accomplish this end and reduce the chasm between education and life. Our children must be prepared to have better conversations about education and life than we currently have. That is what it means to have an evolutionary, indeed a democratic society.

Extension

Developing our teaching practice on our own is certainly possible. We can audio record ourselves and listen to our language through the framework of books like this. We can interview students, listen to what they have to say, and think through its roots in our teaching talk. However, building our own learning communities is a much more productive way to go about it, and much more enjoyable at the same time. Although Vygotsky did not say this, I am sure he would have argued that, like children, teachers grow into the intellectual life around them. I'll call this Johnston's corollary to Vygotsky. All of the language and logic we have explored in this book applies as much to teachers as to students. Just like children, we have to exercise some control over that intellectual environment so that we continue to develop. This requires that we build productive learning communities, with language that reflects the dimensions we have explored in this book. It also requires engaging in open tasks that require us to articulate our thinking. So, now that you have a sense of the dimensions of classroom talk, let's try bringing them together to think through what children have to say. In Chapter 3, you considered an abstract of a conversation with

Mandy (page 36). I have included in Appendix B abstracts of conversations with one of Mandy's classmates and two students from another classroom. With a couple of colleagues, read these abstracts and do the following activities.

Instructions

Read the four mini cases in Appendix B, and:

1 Decide which students are from the same classroom, articulating your logic for each other as you do so. Line by line, imagine what each teacher says that makes it possible for the students to say what they do.

One student in each classroom performs substantially better on reading tests than the other (upper vs. lower quartile in the class). Decide which is which, again articulating your logic

Who Do You Think You're Talking To?

> If we live, we stand in language. You must change your words.
>
> Kendrick Smithyman[1]

Barbara Kingsolver in a short story called "Quality Time" introduces readers to Miriam who finds herself unexpectedly pregnant. Miriam confesses to her sister Janice that "I haven't even worked out what I want to pass on to a child." Janice laughs:

According to Janice, parenting was 3 percent conscious effort and 97 percent automatic pilot. "It doesn't matter what you think you're going to tell them. What matters is they're right there watching you every minute, while you let the lady with just two items go ahead of you in line, or when you lay on the horn and swear at the guy that cuts you off in traffic. There's no sense kidding yourself, what you see is what you get."[2]

Teaching, like parenting, is, for much of the day, automatic. I like to think that in teaching, the proportion of conscious effort is a little higher, particularly in the planning department, but thinking through what we are going to say next *as we interact* with children would mean that we were not giving them our full attention and not being genuine. Children would immediately notice this—the little planning pauses in our speech such as, "That's... nice." To think that children would not notice these is to seriously underestimate their ability to make sense of language. So the question is, what makes it possible for teachers to say the wonderful things they say genuinely, automatically, and consistently?

I say *consistently*, because when we say something, regardless of the meaning we intend, people make sense of it given the immediate situation (as they understand it), their past experience, what has been said before, what is said after, and so forth. Consequently, the messages we convey about noticing, identity, agency, social-emotional life, epistemology, competence, and democratic living have to be consistent threads. We can't get away with isolated words, phrases, and sentences, no matter how wonderful they might appear. We can't use them as teaching tools as if they stand alone and can be picked up and put down at will.

I raise the issue of *genuineness* because we speak as human beings. Our speech is inseparable from our bodies. Its tone, modulation, pitch, and so forth are affected by feelings, attitudes, and relationships. We cannot effectively use a particular kind of language if the body and other crucial indicators give conflicting messages. If we are angry with a child, or disappointed, or think he or she is "learning disabled" or "gifted," we might not directly say it, but there will be traces of it in our speech. Kingsolver's "What you see" is made up of much more than simply the words I have highlighted in this book. The pauses, coughs, sighs, frowns, postures, and so forth are all part of our language, along with the way we organize the classroom, the activities we design, the resources we make available, and so forth. All are part of the *discourse* of the classroom and all interact with one another. Children make sense of language, themselves, and each other in the context of it all.

Of course, consistency and genuineness are aspects of the same thing. The teachers I have described as inviting a productive epistemology invited their students into interesting conversations and were genuinely interested in what they had to say. But they were more generally interested in their students too, not just in the ideas they contributed. They made individual personal contact with them regularly as they arrived at school and during the day, learning what in their lives mattered and what could become relevant for them. This made it easier for them to find a path to enter the same learning space—to generate intersubjectivity. They also arranged for children to come to understand each other in ways that led to a productive intermental space for the class.

Who Do You Think You're Talking To?

Let me use a fairly crude illustration. When we talk to babies, our speech is comically unlike our normal speech. We raise the pitch of our voices, reduce the length of our utterances, and use lots of questions, declaratives, and deictic references (like "that's a book"). We also become repetitive, exaggerate inflection, and use a range of attention-getting strategies. When we talk with dogs, of course, we sound very similar—similar, but not the same.[3] With dogs, our utterances become even shorter. We use declaratives rather than questions, our repetitions are exact rather than varied, and we don't use deictic references. We talk *similarly* to dogs and babies, because we assume that both are inattentive and limited in their capabilities and we want to gain their attention, express affection, and perhaps control their behavior. We talk *differently* to dogs than to babies because we do not expect dogs to become real conversation partners or to grow in their ability to name things and express themselves. In other words, we talk to them differently because of who we think they are and what we think we are doing with them.

For example, at the beginning of the year, Bristol, an eighth grader, seemed "almost hostile" to her teacher, Mr. Simmons.[4] He chalked it up to "She really didn't know me." So he made a point of having conversations with her around the books she was trying out. Quite quickly Bristol's attitude changed—a smile and a comment on entering the classroom, and initiating book conversations with him. This shift would be unlikely if Mr. Simmons had instead viewed her as insolent or threatening his authority. Mr. Simmons's is rigorously persistent with this approach, which is particularly important for his Black students. Had Bristol been Black, for example, he would need to actively resist racial stereotypes pushing him to view her actions as more aggressive, insolent, and punishable.[5]

You've probably had the experience of someone talking to you in a way that makes you think "Who do you think you're talking to?" or, equally, "Who do you think you are?" When this happens to us, they appear to have communicated, by the way they talk to us, who they think we are. We become conscious of it because who *they* think we are conflicts with who *we* think we are. In familiar situations, we have a deep sense of who we are that we have developed in interaction with others over an extended period. Most of the time, we are unaware of the process even as we take our assigned positions in this ongoing dance. The way we interact with children and arrange for them to interact shows them what kinds of people we think they are and gives them opportunities to practice being those kinds of people. We provide them with what James Gee calls an "identity kit."[6]

Let me give you an example. A few years ago, I interviewed a fourth-grade student, Sean. Part of the interview was as follows:[7]

Me: If you had a pen pal in another class and you wanted to find out about him as a reader, what kind of questions would you ask?

Sean: Maybe ask them what reading level you read at...

Me: Are there different kinds of readers in your class?

Sean: There's ones like the people who's not good and the people who are good...

Me: When you are discussing as a group do you like to contribute?

Sean: Not really. 'Cause I think that what Mrs. Wilson does is right. She sort of starts off easy and then she gets real hard with the questions.

Me: Do you ever disagree with the other kids with those discussions?

Sean: No. 'Cause they usually be right.

There is no mistaking who Sean thinks he is in this context, and he didn't make it up out of thin air. He had help from the discourse of the classroom. Notice how he feels that the way he has been positioned, and now positions himself, is perfectly normal and appropriate.

I want to stress that Sean's teacher was not mean, quite the reverse. She was a very caring person who liked Sean very much and was attentive to him, and he liked her in return. We can certainly see traces of good/not good reader and ability "levels" in the conversation. But we can also see that it's not simply the names and labels we invoke that affect children, or for that matter the love with which we embrace them, but the ways we *unwittingly* use language to position them and provide them with the means to name and maim *themselves*, as we saw in Chapter 5. I have dedicated this book to the possibility that we can *wittingly* use the same principles to do the reverse—provide children with the means and the desire to construct themselves as responsibly literate democratic citizens. However, I must emphasize that the teachers whose language we have explored in this book used that language mostly without conscious attention to it, just as Barbara Kingsolver's Janice expected they would. They can do this, in part, because of who they think they and the children are, but also because of what they think they are doing.

What Do You Think You're Doing?

In the course of our research, we interviewed a teacher who explained that in her class they do their reading aloud, "for me to be sure that they have truly read it... which in some ways isn't fair to the students who have high skills because they could be going further."[8] She also noted with regard to discussing books, there are "so few that actually stay engaged... with the conversation, that I don't use it too often... They're very good if I'm leading the discussion... they're not good at making choices." It's fairly easy to hear the way Pam thinks of her students. They are people who cannot be trusted or expected to read independently or to make productive choices, children who are incapable of having a conversation. Her students also come in varieties of more and less capable, and the more capable ones are those who are "good at listening, following directions, ... following through and doing a good job." With regard to students' different understandings of books, she observed that, "I'm more concerned with writing it and correcting it and making sure I explain it to them... They tend to be very accepting of problems or explanations... they don't question too often." Pam's stance toward her students is hierarchical and separate. She makes a fairly clear I/they distinction, rather than a collective we. She has the knowledge, and expertise to deliver it to the students, and makes sure she does so. She is the sole authority and her job is to make sure that her students get things right.

In other words, as Pam talks about her teaching she makes clear who she thinks she is talking to, who she thinks she is, and the nature of the activity they are engaged in. She conveys all of this in her interactions with her students. To verify this, check the transcript example on page 86–87, which came from her classroom. Pam's students like her, and her teaching helps them perform better than average on standardized tests. However, what they learn about literacy, and themselves, and each other as literate individuals—concepts not represented on standardized tests—is very different from students in certain other classrooms. It's different *because* of the way Pam quite genuinely and consistently uses language with her students. She uses language this way because of the way she thinks of herself and her students and what they are doing.

A teacher who held different views would use different language. Take Stacey for example.[9] Stacey's goal is that her students will be "independent thinkers" who "question every single thing." She insists on children discussing ideas in their books and wants them to respect one another and know "that there are going to be differences of opinion but we respect them." For her, it's important that authority in the classroom is distributed so that students can become independent, not only in terms of self-management, but in terms of their learning and thinking. She wants her students to be independent and "involved in the decision making," and to "reflect... [on] what's working and what's not [and] what we can do to change those things that are not working." Stacey wants her students to think of reading as "an opportunity to take themselves to another place, as an opportunity to think... a commitment to themselves as thinkers." A successful reader in her class "looks at reading with reader's eyes in terms of reflective thinking, and then she sees it with author's eyes in terms of intentions—what did the author intend? Why?"

Listening to Stacey talk about her students and what they are doing, we hear a very different view of who she thinks the students are and what she thinks they are doing together. She does not view her students hierarchically and she does not think of teaching in terms of delivery. Literacy and learning are in order to do things rather than an end in themselves. She is clear that students have to take responsibility for their learning and the knowledge they construct and that her job is to help them do that. She does not describe students in terms of good and bad, but in terms of interests.

Are these ways of thinking evident in her teaching interactions? Absolutely. Several of the examples I have used in the earlier chapters come from Stacey's room. When she says, "So, friends, as a writer that's what decisions you have to make," it's because she believes that's what writers do and because she views the people she is talking to as writers.[10] Are these differences reflected in her students' views of themselves? See if you can pick from the four cases in Appendix B which ones come from Stacey's room and which ones come from Pam's. Remember to do it with a colleague and to articulate your reasoning to each other.

Ways of Thinking: Ways of Interacting

My point is that these teachers have very different ways of thinking about who they are, who their students are, and what they think they are doing, and these ways of thinking strongly influence the language they use automatically. Consider first-grade teacher Debbie Miller.[11] When Debbie says to her students as they leave at the end of the day, "Thanks for coming," she could have planned to say that in advance. Of course, the students would know whether or not she was being genuine because of the comment's consistency with the rest of the classroom discourse. However, she could not plan the following interaction when Brendan shares with the class what happened when he read a particular non-fiction book:

Debbie: (To Brendan) Can I tell the other really brilliant thing that you did?
(To the class) Brendan had read this book before but what he did was he just picked it up again right? And then, when he read it again, he said, "I never knew this. This is a poem." The first time he read it and the second time and the third time he was just thinking about learning the words and figuring out the words, right Brendan? But, then, this time, he made this big discovery that it's actually written as a... [Students fill in "poem"] and who would have thought that a non-fiction book could actually be poetry? He learned that today, and that's because I think he had read it before.
Brendan: And Mrs. Miller didn't know that (big smile).
Debbie: I didn't know that, and you taught that to me. It was... I wrote it right down here in my notebook. Thank you, Brendan.

I assume that, by this point, you are doing your own analysis of interactions, but just in case you are interested in my interpretation of this interaction, go to Appendix C. The main thing I would highlight is the consistency within the interaction in terms of epistemological stance. Debbie could not fake this interaction and the many such interactions during the day that are consistent with it on so many levels (like the other example from her classroom on page 96), because they happen on the spot, without planning time, and they happen over and over again. How does she do it?

In an interview, here's how Debbie explains what she is doing when she arranges reading discussions among the children:[12]

> I'm not concerned so much as to the content of what they're saying really, I mean I'm interested in that, but I'm really interested in "so what did you notice about yourself as a learner when you were talking with somebody?" … I mean I want to make that broader leap… What kinds of new ideas can you learn from somebody else? Did you find out something or did you learn something that you didn't know before? …
>
> When I ask them to go eye-to-eye and knee-to-knee [to discuss], [it] is just to give them more experience actually accessing what they know and being able to articulate it in a way it makes sense to somebody else and then to build on each other's thinking. And so that's… you know, I think even, the bigger idea.

What she thinks she is doing is getting children to understand that they have something to say, and that engaging with others is in their own developmental interests in terms of what they can learn about the world and about themselves as learners, and the thoughts they can entertain. She wants them to treat each other with that in mind. She wants them to be aware of themselves as learners, and how they actually do what they do. Her language is primarily a reflection of these goals. If we want to change our words, we need to change our views.

Changing Our Words and Keeping Our Heads Up

Although the genuineness and consistency these teachers show in their interactions with students lies in these deeper beliefs, I think we can start to change our classroom interactions by changing our words and dragging some of our beliefs along with them. The language I have suggested throughout the book is likely to result in changes in other aspects of the classroom dynamic. For example, just saying, "How did you..." or "How else?" or "Did anyone notice..." are ways of starting useful conversations that can be consciously applied with little complication. Certainly, reflecting back to students the things they are doing well can be instituted with substantial effect and minimal additional requirements. We just have to make it a priority, and we might have to consciously edit our speech for a bit. We can also make it clear to students that we are interested in what they have to say. If you tried the exercises at the end of Chapter 7, I hope you found this to be the case.

However, making major change in our language is difficult without having other supports in place. Most importantly, unless what the children are doing in school is meaningful, that is, relevant to their immediate lives and goals, they will easily help us to shift back into unproductive language. Indeed, many of the comments we have discussed in the book can be seen as vehicles for making learning meaningful to students, and students productively meaningful to themselves and each other. As Vygotsky pointed out, meaningfulness is what makes it possible for children to interact in productive ways, and to be in control of their learning, integrating the connections among thinking, acting, and feeling. Without meaningful activity, children do not develop internal control.[13] Yet, pressures of testing and overstuffed curricula easily make us abandon meaningfulness and reduce our view of our work to mere individual cognitive skill building. It's easy to forget the need to engage the whole person in joint community activities that are socially and personally meaningful and emotionally satisfying.

To be meaningful, teaching children to become literate is about the here and now, and what children can do with literacy to serve their interests. However, for us, it's at least as much about the society we wish for our children and who we wish our children to become. The possibility of an evolutionary democratic society depends on children's understandings of who they are (and might become), their epistemological understandings, what they take to be normal relationships with others, and the narratives they can imagine for themselves. We can keep the tests and other potentially distracting elements in mind, but we have to keep our heads up further than that as we deal with the moment-to-moment interactions with students. In a tense, emotionally charged situation, for example, with no time for planning, Tracy says to a student:

Feelings are hurt and so because you don't deal with them, you... you walk away being angry, and I don't want that to happen... you know... it wasn't your intention to hurt his feelings but you were angry. I'm just trying to get you to understand why he would respond the way he did and why you would respond the way you did... I don't want to invalidate how you are feeling... just understand why you are feeling the way you do... then we'll all have a better understanding of one another.[14]

Tracy's goal is not merely to deal with the immediate situation. She has a larger goal in mind. Perhaps I should say that she is dealing with the immediate situation within a larger frame of reference—an activity and goal structure that saturate her language choices. She is addressing these cranky students within the same principles she holds for her literacy instruction. It's her belief that understanding ourselves entails understanding others and how we are alike and not alike, and our intentions, our thoughts, and our feelings. This, in turn, requires active mind reading so that we can readily see others in ourselves and ourselves in others. In this line of thinking, the more we understand each other as extensions of ourselves, and difference as potential for our own development, the more critically literate we will be and, as Mary Rose O'Reilly would have it, the less likely we are to kill one another. Indeed, that is part of what Tracy thinks she is doing. She is coaching children to interact with each other in ways that will lead to positive relationships and selves, not just for the sake of a caring classroom learning community, though there is that, but for life.

Robert Young observes that we are "entitled to ask of any view of human learning and inquiry: 'What image of humanity is inherent in it?'"[15] I hope the contrasting examples I have provided in this chapter have encouraged you to do this. I hope I have also convinced you that exploring the image of humanity inherent in the language of our teaching is not merely a fascination. It's a responsibility. I know the image I stand with. I stand with Mary Rose O'Reilly, Joan, Debbie, Tracy, and the many other teachers whose words I have shown you, working for a society we can *live* with.

When I say *live with*, I don't only mean in the sense of not being killed, but with the understanding that to live means to grow, and failure to grow intellectually and socially is not living, but merely existing. In my view, the real beauty in these teachers' classroom talk is that they show us that teaching toward such a society does not entail compromising more narrowly academic ends. We can have our cake and eat it too (and it's delicious).

The Fine Print

People may get an education from reading the fine print, but what they get from not reading it is usually experience.

Vesta M. Kelly[1]

In order to begin writing this book, I needed to get to the point as quickly as possible, so I took a few liberties—I swept a few details about language under the rug. By choosing to read this appendix you have lifted the rug, so I must assume that you're interested in those details, even if they're a bit messier than the tidied-up version of language I presented in the rest of the book. In some ways, you might view this appendix as the fine print—the "some restrictions apply" and "void where prohibited" clauses.

Language turns out to be a very tricky tool for communication. Although I have written much of this book as if particular words and phrases have specific meanings, words by themselves mean nothing—only what the social context allows them to say. Whatever is said before, or after, will change the meaning. For example, the meaning of "good," said in response to a student's work, will be changed by saying "fantastic" to the next student.

Even saying nothing can mean different things. Although I present "wait time" in Chapter 8 as if it means one thing, its meaning will depend on where it occurs in a conversation between which people. You can probably imagine a conversation in which a silence means, "I don't think I believe you," another in which it means "You win," another in which it means "How dare you," and still another which means "You really disappointed me." Each of these will be accompanied by different body positions and facial expressions. A silence will also feel different depending on who is present in the room and their social standing in relation to one another. In other words, in order to understand what someone is saying we have to make a bunch of assumptions about the circumstances—who the person thinks they are, who they think we are, what sort of interaction this is, and so forth.

Generating these shared meanings (communicating) is accomplished not only through language, but also through a range of other cultural tools like facial expression, gesture, voice tone, and spatial arrangements. To complicate things further, each of us carries around in our bodies a history of the interactions in which we have been involved—what Pierre Bourdieu called habitus.[2] Silence will *feel* different (mean different things) to people with different cultural histories and in different contexts. The meaning of language depends, too, on the relational context. Without trust and respect many of the examples I provide in the book become quite unpredictable. At its heart, teaching is a culturally, socially, and emotionally engaging process. Teachers who find what children do and say interesting are able to scaffold classroom learning and bridge cultural complexities by spinning appreciative narratives for children. The listening and the narratives create the necessary "atmosphere of approval" and trust.[3]

Cultural Complexities

Children often bring very different cultural assumptions about how adults and children interact. For example, children used to very direct language might be puzzled when they encounter indirect requests such as "Would you like to open your books now?" Children have different expectations about how boys and girls should interact, and there are regional differences in socially appropriate behavior. For example, the length of time people wait to be sure that someone has finished what they are saying is very much shorter in New York City, say, than in rural New York.[4]

It will behoove us to be sensitive to the cultural variations present in our classrooms (and there might be many) so we don't react poorly to the interpretations children make. It might be worth remembering that treating interactional problems as ones of misinterpretation is a much safer default than treating them as willful disobedience. Although in this book I have minimally addressed the cultural and linguistic variation we encounter in classrooms, the epistemological stance I have favored throughout is more culturally permeable as well as more generally productive.[5]

Overlaps, Common Themes, and Other Liberties

While I am in confessional mode, I should say that I have also taken some liberties with the ideas of agency and narrative that I present in Chapter 4. For example, I have written as if there is only one kind of narrative. Of course, there are many. There are class, gender, and cultural differences in the ways people tell personal narratives. This can produce misunderstandings when children tell stories in class that do not fit the narrative form we expect.[6] Sometimes we have to tune our ears to these cultural differences, perhaps using local cultural representatives such as parents to help us. However, of equal significance from my perspective are the narrative differences that lead to inequities. For example, some cultures do not pass on the same narrative possibilities to boys and girls. In school, we try to help children open possibilities by restructuring the narratives they have available. This is also part of counseling practice.[7] If this seems like tampering with people's cultures, it is. This is one of the many reasons why teaching is a political activity.

I have taken similar liberties with the concept of agency. What I refer to as a sense of agency,[8] others have referred to as self-efficacy,[9] or a sense of control or effectance.[10] These concepts are not all identical but, in my view, they have more than enough in common to make this conflation reasonable for practice. Some of my suggestions regarding agency and narrative have also come from a field called attribution theory—the study of people's attributions for successful and unsuccessful experiences.[11] Though these fields are different, they overlap a great deal and address much the same thing—the stories children use to make sense of their experience.

There is actually a lot of overlap among different domains of research. Indeed, although I have separated teachers' language use into different chapters to emphasize different dimensions, the obvious overlap among both categories and consequences shouldn't surprise us. We can see this from research with younger children. For example, research into parent–child interactions tells us that children who have a greater sense of agency likely experienced warm and caring home environments emphasizing independence.[12] Children with a weaker sense of agency are more likely to have experienced critical or punitive environments.[13] These sorts of conclusions fit well with what I discuss in the book, and when people coming at things from different directions arrive at similar conclusions, the overlaps and consistencies offer us more confidence.

I should make one final note on the term "discourse" which I use here and there in the book referring to the broader communicative context of which talk is but one facet. The clearest, and probably most widely quoted, definition of discourse is that provided by James Gee:[14]

> Discourses are ways of being in the world, or forms of life which integrate words, acts, values, beliefs, attitudes, and social identities, as well as gestures, glances, body positions, and clothes. A Discourse is a sort of identity kit which comes complete with the appropriate costume and instructions on how to act, talk, and often write, so as to take on a particular social role that others will recognize.

You will see that I have focused on various parts of discourse throughout the book and ignored others. In Chapter 10, I described how talk, values, beliefs, attitudes, and identities fit together, so I will refer you to that chapter for more detail.

Four Fourth Graders

These four "cases" are adapted from "Teaching and learning literate epistemologies."[1]

Mandy

Mandy says that a good writer "writes fast. [For example] when the teacher tells us to write a story then it doesn't even take her not even ten minutes." Mandy does not talk with other students about their writing. She "wouldn't want to hurt their feelings or nothing because sometimes when someone comes up to them and says, 'Oh, you're a bad writer,' and everything. Then, they'll tell the teacher." Mandy says that they should not give other students ideas, "because then that would be giving them things that you thought of in your head. Then they'll have, probably, the same stories."

Good readers, she says, are "all the kids that are quiet and they just listen... they challenge themselves, they get chapter books." Asked to describe herself as a reader or a writer, she says she doesn't understand the question. She does not know how she could learn about another child as a reader or writer.

Asked whether they do research in her class, she says she is unsure what it is. When it is explained, she says they don't do it. Mandy expects on her report card an "excellent" for writing and a comment like, "Mandy has behaved and she is nice to other classmates." To help a classmate become a better reader, she would tell them to "stop fooling around because the more you fool around, the more you get your name on the board and checks... [and] if he doesn't know that word, if he doesn't know how to sound it out or if he doesn't know what it means, look it up in the dictionary."

In talking about books, Mandy makes no connections across books or with personal experience (pp. 226–227).

Steven

As a writer, Steven is confident about the significance of his own experience and the experiences of others. He uses these in his writing to figure out audience and characters. He took three weeks to write one of his pieces, including "some really hard struggles" (said with relish). In a reflection about a piece of writing he says, "But then I said to myself, well, where's a place that gets the reader in good suspense so they want to read on, but it's a good stopping place?" And, "So I was looking at it and I'm like, well, how can I say that this statue, I mean that this trophy is really important to me. And how can I make it... make that word 'trophy' be more symbolized in the statue. And I based it on the trophy, but it was really about a statue."

What he does well as a writer is "express my feelings well" and "really get out what I want to say," but sometimes he gets "into a staring match with a blank page."

In his research on racial segregation in airports, he tried two different libraries and the internet, and called the local airport. He has not encountered discrepant information sources yet, but if he did, he would "take those two opinions and put them together and then I would have a variety of what one author thought and what the other author thought. So I would just put them together... and see what I came up with... or perhaps try to even it out."

Asked whether there are any good authors in his class, he says, "For the funny part, Jessie is really funny. He writes a lot about fantasy stuff... Ron's a pretty good writer... and he's a little better at drawing than writing... Emily [in her mystery] gave details. She described the characters. It was a really good mystery because it had a point and it had something that the reader had to figure out." He has a great deal of knowledge about the structure of different genres—realistic fiction, fantasy, mystery, and biography, among others. Commenting on his own piece, he says, "Unlike most mysteries it has a sad ending."

He routinely makes connections among the books he reads and has specific criteria for what he appreciates about particular books (p. 229).

Henry

Describing himself as a writer, Henry says he's "Typical. I don't, like, ... finish a final copy and start writing another story right away. It takes me a little longer. I write a lot of stuff that's happened to me. Like, I have entries about like when I was at the beach with my friends, or I can borrow [ideas]." The most recent thing he learned as a writer is "how to be more organized," and next he would like to learn how to write longer stories because "I have lots of information. I know I've got more."

Conferences with friends, he says, "give me, like, ideas to put in there [or] they think it's good, it's got enough details and stuff then I could meet with the teacher." Asked whether there are different kinds of readers in his class, he says, "Like Steve, he reads longer books than other people. And Dan. When he gets into a book, you're not going to stop him, like if you say, 'Hey, Dan, listen to this sentence.' He's not going to come out of that book. Jenny, she reads hard books like Steve. But, umm, she finishes books, like, really fast. Priscilla. She really likes to read mysteries. She reads long stories, like Nancy Drew." He also notes that, like him, Roger enjoys the Bailey School Kids books. To learn about a pen pal as a reader, he would ask, "What kind of books do you like? Who's your favorite author? What book are you reading now? ... Have you read any good books lately?"

To help a classmate become a better reader: "If they are reading harder books that are too hard for them, [tell them] not to push themselves as much. Maybe later in a couple of months read those books. Push them to the side and read, like, books that are at your level."

Henry enjoys adding to class discussions of books. "Like Mrs. Hopkins says when we are in the literature group, I always have something to relate to the book." He finds other students' experiences and interpretations of the book interesting, except "If they talk about some of the really little details that you don't really need." He feels comfortable disagreeing with other students and quotes what he said to a classmate on a particular occasion. He enjoys reading, and often makes connections between books. He also thinks some of the students in the class are good authors, because, for example, when "Emelia read hers... it was really long, but I'm like, what's going to happen next? Once you get into it you want to know what's going to happen next. Their mysteries are really a mystery." This is not always true with commercial books. "Like it says the 'Boxcar Children Mysteries' on the front of the book and it says the mystery of the missing something... and then, like, I can't get the mystery out of it. It just doesn't give it to you."

When he encounters conflicts among books when researching a topic, he says that one of the authors "probably hadn't done his homework." His strategy for dealing with such situations is to consult more sources (pp. 228–229).

Millie

Millie chose *Superfudge* to read "because it was, like, challenging, the words that was in there. Because we don't read that book until fifth grade and I was going to try it." She likes realistic fiction, though she does not have a term for describing it. She thinks that as a reader, "I'm not all perfect in reading. But I'm good. But I mess up a lot because when you mess up, you learn from your mistakes."

Asked whether there are different readers in her class, she uses a good/not-good continuum and levels: "Well, they can read more better than me because when they read, they don't mess up as much as I do... they are on a higher level than me." She says that she has changed as a reader "because I'm reading more and more and bigger stories than last year." What she would like to learn next is to "learn books harder than chapter books so I can almost get on a higher level." She likes to add to discussions when they have them. For example, the class disagreed on whether the author of *Stone Fox* should have let Searchlight die. She never disagrees with the teacher.

Her best piece of writing she thinks took fifteen to twenty minutes, and she selected it because "We had to write what does responsibility mean and I won." Asked what she does well as a writer, she says, "People tell me that when I write, I write good because I say what I want to say, not what somebody else says. I don't take people's ideas. I just think of my own and just write." The thing she learned most recently about writing is that "if you write and you copy off of somebody that means you're not... you're acting like you're not a real writer. 'Cause if you were a real writer, you would think of your own ideas to make your own story." Her friend is a good author because she "tells examples and she makes her stories long."

To help someone with writing: "If they need help, or in spelling... in cursive I would give them 'cause I have sheets, spelling sheets that you can trace and stuff... and they can practice." Asked whether they do research in her class she says, "The research we do, like if we need a word that we don't know what it means, we will look it up in a dictionary." She has never encountered conflicting sources of information (p. 227).

Analysis of Debbie Miller's Interaction with the Class and Brendan

Debbie Miller's Comments	Analysis
DM: Can I tell the other really brilliant thing that you did?	Asks student's permission to share his skill and knowledge, thus maintaining his authority. "Really brilliant" might have pointed to a less helpful stable characteristic such as "smart," but here it is associated with the strategies used, making it smart to use strategies.

Debbie Miller's Comments	Analysis
Brendan had read this book before, but what he did was, he just picked it up again,	It is okay to reread books.
right?	Checking with the authority to make sure the story is accurate from his point of view, reminding the class, and Brendan, of his authority.
And then, when he read it again, he said, "I never knew this. This is a poem" ...	When we reread, we can notice new things in part because our focus is different. One thing to notice is poetry.
The first time he read it and the second time and the third time he was just thinking about learning the words and figuring out the words,	Reading something a lot can be useful. Notice what happens in your mind when you read.
right, Brendan?	Checking with the authority to make sure the story is accurate from his point of view, reminding the class, and Brendan, of his authority.
But then, this time, he made this big discovery that it's actually written as a... [poem].	Be sure to notice surprises because they are often important, new information. Pauses invite children's participation in the reconstructed think-aloud.

(*Continued*)

Debbie Miller's Comments	Analysis
...who would have thought that a non-fiction book could actually be poetry?	Reminder of surprise and its significance, both the immediate learning and for future possibilities.
He learned that today, and that's because I think he had read it before.	Rereading often leads to new learning.
B: And Mrs. Miller didn't know that (big smile).	Brendan recognizes his own authority, his own agency, along with the feeling of associated pride. Understands that children can teach teachers, and the underlying principle of distributed cognition.
DM: I didn't know that, and you taught that to me.	Affirms student's successful learning and his teaching, and reaffirms that teachers don't know everything.
I wrote it right down here in my notebook.	Additional affirmation, again asserting the student's authority.
Thank you, Brendan.	One final mark of respect for the student, and of the value placed on learning.

Notes

Chapter 1: The Language of Influence in Teaching

1 Johnston and Ivey. "Classroom talk and individual differences in reading." p. 214.
2 Vygotsky. *Mind in society: The development of higher psychological processes.* p. 88.
3 O'Reilley. *The peaceable classroom.* p. 30.
4 Wharton-McDonald, Boothroyd, and Johnston. *Students' talk about readers and writers, reading and writing.* p. 201.
5 Johnston, Bennett, and Cronin. "Literate achievements in fourth grade." p. 194.
6 Wharton-McDonald, Boothroyd, and Johnston. *Students' talk about readers and writers, reading and writing.* p. 2.
7 Crum and Langer. "Mind-set matters: Exercise and the placebo effect."
8 Rio and Alvarez. "From activity to directivity: The question of involvement in education."
   Scollon. "Mediated discourse and social interaction."
9 Halliday. *An introduction to functional grammar.*
10 Pressley, Allington, Wharton-MacDonald, Collins-Block, and Morrow. *Learning to read: Lessons from exemplary first-grade classrooms.*
   Delpit. "The silenced dialogue: Power and pedagogy in educating other people's children."
   Pressley and Woloshyn. *Cognitive strategy instruction that really improves children's academic performance.*
   Naraian, "Teaching for 'real': Reconciling explicit literacy instruction with inclusive pedagogy in a fourth-grade urban classroom."
   McGinty, Justice, Piasta, Kaderavek, and Fan, "Does context matter? Explicit print instruction during reading varies in its influence by child and classroom factors."
11 Clay. *Becoming literate: The construction of inner control.*
12 Donaldson. *Children's minds.*

13 Grice. "Logic and conversation."

14 Grice. "Logic and conversation."

15 Allington and Johnston. *Reading to learn: Lessons from exemplary fourth-grade classrooms.*

Johnston, Guice, Baker, Malone, and Michelson. "Assessment of teaching and learning in 'literature based' classrooms."

16 Taylor, Peterson, Pearson, and Rodriguez. "Looking inside classrooms: Reflecting on the 'how' as well as the 'what' in effective reading instruction."

Sun, Anderson, Lin, Morris, Miller, Ma, Thi Nguyen-Jahiel, and Scott. "Children's engagement during collaborative learning and direct instruction through the lens of participant structure."

17 I am not using these constructs as a dichotomy, or even as a continuum. Many researchers use these as different, though not entirely independent dimensions.

18 Kondo. *Crafting selves: Power, gender, and discourses of identity in a Japanese workplace.*

19 Austin. *How to do things with words.*

20 Davies and Harre. "Positioning and personhood."

Langenhove and Harre. "Introducing positioning theory."

21 Langer. *The power of mindful learning.*

22 Luria. *The working brain.*

Neisser. *Cognition and reality: Principles and implications of cognitive psychology.*

Barrett. *How emotions are made: The secret life of the brain.*

23 Harre and Gillet. *The discursive mind.* p. 169.

24 Reichenbach. "The postmodern self and the problem of developing a democratic mind."

25 Davies and Harre. "Positioning and personhood." p. 38.

Chapter 2: Noticing and Naming

1 Halliday. "Towards a language-based theory of learning." p. 94.

2 Langer. *The power of mindful learning.* p. 62.

3 Langer. *Mindfulness.*

4 Harre and Gillet. *The discursive mind.*

5 Barrett. *How emotions are made: The secret life of the brain.*

6 Gauvain. *The social context of cognitive development.* p. 70.

7 Johnston, Champeau, Hartwig, Helmer, Komar, Krueger, and McCarthy. *Engaging literate minds: Developing children's social, emotional, and intellectual lives, K-3.*

8 Clay. *Reading recovery: A guidebook for teachers in training.*

9 Eder. "Comments on children's self-narratives."

10 Bandura. "Self-efficacy: Toward a unifying theory of behavioral change."

11 Johnston, Bennett, and Cronin. "'I want students who are thinkers.'" p. 150.

12 Johnston and Backer. "Inquiry and a good conversation: 'I learn a lot from them.'" p. 44.

13 Repacholi. "Infant's use of attentional cues to identify the referent of another person's emotional expression."

14 Allington and Johnston. "Integrated instruction in exemplary fourth-grade classrooms." p. 181.

   Johnston and Backer. "Inquiry and a good conversation: 'I learn a lot from them.'" p. 181.

15 Adams. *A descriptive study of second graders' conversations about books.* p. 115.

16 Dunham, Dunham, and Curwin. "Joint-attentional states and lexical acquisition at 18 months."

   Tomasello and Farrar. "Joint attention and early language."

   I say "mothers" here rather than parents, because research on these matters is done with mothers and it's hard to know whether the same applies to fathers because sometimes fathers' behaviors affect children differently from those of mothers.

17 Schaffer. "Joint involvement episodes as context for development."

18 Brashares. *The second summer of the sisterhood.*

19 Johnston. "Unpacking literate 'achievement.'" p. 30.

20 Johnston. *Opening minds: Using language to change lives.* p. 2.

21 Campbell. "Stereotyped at seven? Biases in teacher judgement of pupils' ability and attainment."

   Papandrea, Namazi, Ghanim, and Patten, "Identifying racial and socioeconomic biases in New Jersey special education eligibility."

22 Wallis, "Unequal surgery." p. 30.

   Akinade, Kheyfets, Piverger, Layne, Howell, and Janevic. "The influence of racial-ethnic discrimination on women's health care outcomes: A mixed methods systematic review."

23 Kelly, Quinn, Slater, Lee, Gibson, Smith, Ge, and Pascalis. "Three-month-olds, but not newborns, prefer own-race faces."

24 Baron. "Constraints on the development of implicit intergroup attitudes."

25 Garg, Schiebinger, Jurafsky, and Zou. "Word embeddings quantify 100 years of gender and ethnic stereotypes."

   Hauser and Schwarz, "Implicit bias reflects the company that words keep."

Charlesworth, Yang, Mann, Kurdi, and Banaji. "Gender stereotypes in natural language: Word embeddings show robust consistency across child and adult language corpora of more than 65 million words."

Lewis, Cooper Borkenhagen, Converse, Lupyan, and Seidenberg. "What might books be teaching young children about gender?"

26 Charlesworth, Yang, Mann, Kurdi, and Banaji. "Gender stereotypes in natural language: Word embeddings show robust consistency across child and adult language corpora of more than 65 million words."

Lewis, Cooper Borkenhagen, Converse, Lupyan, and Seidenberg. "What might books be teaching young children about gender?"

27 Caliskan and Lewis. "Social biases in word embeddings and their relation to human cognition."

28 WVTM13. *Voters erase racist wording in Alabama Constitution.*

Chapter 3: Identity

1 Dyson and Genishi. "Introduction: The need for story." p. 4.

2 Johnston, Bennett, and Cronin. "Literate achievements in fourth grade." p. 195.

3 Gee and Gee. "Games as distributed teaching and learning systems." p. 19.

4 Ray and Cleaveland. *About the authors: Writing workshops with our youngest writers.* pp. 10–11.

5 Bruner. "The 'remembered' self."
Bruner. "Life as narrative."
Harre and Gillet. *The discursive mind.*
Randall. *The stories we are.*

6 Ray and Cleaveland. *About the authors: Writing workshops with our youngest writers.* p. 17.

7 Ivey and Johnston. *Teens choosing to read: Fostering social, emotional and intellectual growth through books.*

8 Pontecorvo and Sterponi. "Learning to argue and reason through discourse in educational settings."

9 Fivush. "Constructing narrative, emotion, and self in parent-child conversations about the past."

10 Bruner. "The 'remembered' self."

11 Elbers and Streefland. "'Shall we be researchers again?' Identity and social interaction in a community of inquiry." p. 39.

12 Elbers and Streefland. "'Shall we be researchers again?' Identity and social interaction in a community of inquiry." p. 41.

13 Gee. *Social linguistics and literacies: Ideology in discourses.*

14 Elbers and Streefland. "'Shall we be researchers again?' Identity and social interaction in a community of inquiry." p. 37.

15 Williams and Desteno. "Pride and perseverance: The motivational role of pride."

16 Tracy and Robins. "The psychological structure of pride: A tale of two facets."

17 Cheng, Tracy, Kingstone, Foulsham, and Henrich. "Two ways to the top: Evidence that dominance and prestige are distinct yet viable avenues to social rank and influence."

18 Voina and Stoica. "Reframing leadership: Jacinda Ardern's response to the Covid-19 pandemic."

19 Chang and Sue. "The effects of race and problem type on teachers' assessments of student behavior."

20 Steele and Aronson. "Stereotype threat and the intellectual test performance of African Americans."

21 Ambady, Shih, Kim, and Pittinsky. "Stereotype susceptibility in children: Effects of identity activation on quantitative performance."

22 FitzGerald, Martin, Berner, and Hurst. "Interventions designed to reduce implicit prejudices and implicit stereotypes in real world contexts: A systematic review."

23 Shih, Wang, Bucher, and Stotzer. "Perspective taking: Reducing prejudice towards general outgroups and specific individuals."

24 Rahman. *Disability language guide.*

National Center on Disability and Journalism. "Resources."

Nović. "The harmful ableist language you unknowingly use."

25 National Center for Education Statistics. "Race and ethnicity of public school teachers and their students."

26 Wood, Bruner, and Ross. "The role of tutoring in problem solving." p. 92.

27 Lee. *Culture, literacy, and learning: Taking bloom in the midst of the whirlwind.*

Moll. "Elaborating funds of knowledge: Community-oriented practices in international contexts."

28 NEA Center for Social Justice. "7 harmful racial discourse practices to avoid."

Kay and Orr. *We're gonna keep on talking: How to lead meaningful race conversations in the elementary classroom.*

Kay. *Not light, but fire: How to lead meaningful race conversations in the classroom.*

Michael. *Raising race questions: Whiteness and inquiry in education.*

Stevenson. *Promoting racial literacy in schools: Differences that make a difference.*

Chapter 4: Agency and Becoming Strategic

1 Dyson. "Coach Bombay's kids learn to write: Children's appropriation of media material for school literacy." pp. 396–397.
2 Bandura's "self-efficacy" is the same as what I've called a sense of agency.
3 Bandura. "Self-efficacy: Toward a unifying theory of behavioral change."
   Skinner, Zimmer-Gembeck, and Connell. *Individual differences and the development of perceived control.*
4 Paavola, Kunnari, and Moilanen. "Maternal responsiveness and infant intentional communication: Implications for the early communicative and linguistic development."
   Shannon, Tamis-LeMonda, and Cabrera. "Fathering in infancy: Mutuality and stability between 8 and 16 months."
5 Vallotton. "Do infants influence their quality of care? Infants' communicative gestures predict caregivers' responsiveness."
6 Seligman. *Helplessness: On depression, development, and death.*
   Skinner, Zimmer-Gembeck, and Connell. *Individual differences and the development of perceived control.*
7 Feldman. "Infant–mother and infant–father synchrony: The coregulation of positive arousal."
   Koch, Pascalis, Vivian, Meurer Renner, Murray, and Arteche. "Effects of male postpartum depression on father–infant interaction: The mediating role of face processing."
   Pearson, Melotti, Heron, Joinson, Stein, Ramchandani, and Evans. "Disruption to the development of maternal responsiveness? The impact of prenatal depression on mother–infant interactions."
8 Riessman. *Narrative analysis.* p. 2.
9 Bruner. "The 'remembered' self."
10 Clay. *Becoming literate: The construction of inner control.*
11 Rittle-Johnson. "Promoting transfer: Effects of self-explanation and direct instruction."
12 Cazden. "Revealing and telling: The socialization of attention in learning to read and write."
13 Clay. *Change over time in children's literacy development.*
14 Clay. *Becoming literate: The construction of inner control.*
15 Ellen Langer. *Mindfulness.*
16 Clay. *Change over time in children's literacy development.*
17 Graves. *A fresh look at writing.*
18 Johnston, Bennett, and Cronin. "'I want students who are thinkers.'" p. 155.

19 White and Carlson. "What would Batman do? Self-distancing improves executive function in young children."

White, Prager, Schaefer, Kross, Duckworth, and Carlson. "The "Batman effect": Improving perseverance in young children."

20 Adam and Galinsky. "Enclothed cognition."

21 Johnston, Bennett, and Cronin. "'I want students who are thinkers.'" p. 155.

22 Ivey, Johnston, and Cronin. *Process talk and children's sense of literate competence and agency.*

Eder. "Comments on children's self-narratives."

Skinner, Zimmer-Gembeck, and Connell. *Individual differences and the development of perceived control.* p. 220.

23 Lyons, Pinnell, and DeFord. *Partners in learning: Teachers and children in reading recovery.* pp. 162–163 and 151, respectively.

Chapter 5: Meaning-Making Mindsets

1 Ray and Cleaveland. *A teachers' guide to getting started with beginning writers, K-2.* p. 32.

2 Mueller and Dweck. "Praise for intelligence can undermine children's motivation and performance."

3 Miele and Molden. "Naive theories of intelligence and the role of processing fluency in perceived comprehension."

4 Dweck. *Self-theories: Their role in motivation, personality, and development.*

5 Hong, Chiu, Dweck, Lin, and Wan. "Implicit theories, attributions, and coping: A meaning system approach."

Molden and Dweck. "Finding 'meaning' in psychology."

6 Cimpian, Arce, Markman, and Dweck. "Subtle linguistic cues affect children's motivation."

7 There have been recent critiques of the effectiveness of growth mindset interventions. Critiques suggest that the growth mindset is more effective when it is a foundation of classroom instruction rather than simply an intervention that can be in conflict with other classroom practices and policies. It is more effective when students are encouraged to seek challenges and when they have resources and support. Some worry about an over-emphasis on effort. I agree with all those critiques. The arguments I make in this chapter, however, are not undermined by these or other critiques.

8 Hong, Chiu, Dweck, Lin, and Wan. "Implicit theories, attributions, and coping: A meaning system approach."

Nussbaum and Dweck. "Defensiveness versus remediation: Self-theories and modes of self-esteem maintenance."

9 Aronson, Fried, and Good. "Reducing the effects of stereotype threat on African American college students by shaping theories of intelligence."

Claro, Paunesku, and Dweck. "Mindset equals income as a predictor of achievement."

Porter, Catalán Molina, Cimpian, Roberts, Fredericks, Blackwell, and Trzesniewski. "Growth-mindset intervention delivered by teachers boosts achievement in early adolescence."

10 Guthrie and Humenick. "Motivating students to read: Evidence for classroom practices that increase reading motivation and achievement."

Ivey and Broaddus. "'Just plain reading': A survey of what makes students want to read in middle school classrooms."

11 Kamins and Dweck. "Person versus process praise and criticism: Implications for contingent self-worth and coping."

12 Kamins and Dweck. "Person versus process praise and criticism: Implications for contingent self-worth and coping."

13 Brummelman, Thomaes, de Castro, Overbeek and Bushman. "'That's not just beautiful; that's incredibly beautiful!': The adverse impact of inflated praise on children with low self-esteem."

14 Haimovitz, Kratzer, Kenthirarajah, Walton, and Dweck. *The power of "yet": Communicating the potential to improve through subtle cues in feedback.*

15 Day. "'We learn from each other': Collaboration and community in a bilingual classroom." p. 105.

16 Pinsker. "The problem with 'Hey guys.'"

17 Haimovitz and Dweck. "The origins of children's growth and fixed mindsets: New research and a new proposal."

18 Horn and Giacobbe. *Talking, drawing, writing: Lessons for our youngest writers.* p. 103.

19 Sun. *There's no limit: Mathematics teaching for a growth mindset.*

20 Ivey and Johnston. *Teens choosing to read: Fostering social, emotional and intellectual growth through books.*

21 Hooper, Haimovitz, Wright, Murphy, and Yeager. *Creating a classroom incremental theory matters, but it's not as straightforward as you might think: Evidence from a multi-level analysis at ten high schools.*

22 Haimovitz and Dweck. "What predicts children's fixed and growth intelligence mind-sets? Not their parents' views of intelligence but their parents' views of failure."

Rattan, Good, and Dweck. "'It's ok—Not everyone can be good at math': Instructors with an entity theory comfort (and demotivate) students."

23 Adapted from Johnston. *Opening minds: Using language to change lives*. p. 23.
24 Carr, Dweck, and Pauker. "'Prejudiced' behavior without prejudice? Beliefs about the malleability of prejudice affect interracial interactions."
25 Mueller and Dweck. "Praise for intelligence can undermine children's motivation and performance."
26 West, Buckley, Krachman, and Bookman. "Development and implementation of student social-emotional surveys in the CORE districts."
27 Miele and Molden. "Naive theories of intelligence and the role of processing fluency in perceived comprehension."
28 Chiu, Dweck, Tong, and Fu. "Implicit theories and conceptions of morality."
29 Darnon, Muller, Schrager, Pannuzzo, and Butera. "Mastery and performance goals predict epistemic and relational conflict regulation."
30 Levy, Plaks, Hong, Chiu, and Dweck. "Static versus dynamic theories and the perception of Groups: Different routes to different destinations."
31 Nicholls. *The competitive ethos and democratic education*.
32 Lee and Yeager. "Adolescents with an entity theory of personality are more vigilant to social status and use relational aggression to maintain social status."
33 Zhu and Wong. "What matters for adolescent suicidality: Depressive symptoms or fixed mindsets? Examination of cross-sectional and longitudinal associations between fixed mindsets and suicidal ideation."
   Baer, Grant, and Dweck. *Personal goals, dysphoria, and coping strategies*.
34 Levy-Tossman, Kaplan and Assor. "Academic goal orientations, multiple goal profiles, and friendship intimacy among early adolescents."

Chapter 6: Flexibility and Transfer (or Generalizing)

1 Langer and Piper. "The prevention of mindlessness."
2 Beach. "Activity as a mediator of sociocultural change and individual development: The case of school-work transition."
3 Rittle-Johnson. "Promoting transfer: Effects of self-explanation and direct instruction."
4 Allington and Johnston. "Integrated instruction in exemplary fourth-grade classrooms." p. 180.
5 Kuhn, Garcia-Mila, Zohar, and Anderson. *Strategies of knowledge acquisition*.
6 McKinley and Byrne. *One smile*.

7 Lindfors. *Children's inquiry: Using language to make sense of the world.* p. 170.

8 Wharton-McDonald and Williamson. "Focus on the real and make sure it connects to kids' lives." p. 92.

9 Sutton-Smith. "Radicalizing childhood: The multivocal mind." p. 87.

10 Bateson. *Mind and nature: A necessary unity.*

11 Langer. *Mindfulness.* p. 45.
    Langer and Piper. "The prevention of mindlessness."

12 Langer. *The power of mindful learning.* p.29

13 Graves. *A fresh look at writing.*

14 Sutton-Smith. "Radicalizing childhood: The multivocal mind." p. 71.

15 Steig. *The amazing bone.*

16 Anderson. *How's it going: A practical guide to conferring with student writers.* pp. 77–78.

Chapter 7: Emotional and Social Life

1 Immordino-Yang and Gotlieb. "Embodied brains, social minds, cultural meaning: Integrating neuroscientific and educational research on social-affective development."

2 Barrett. "The theory of constructed emotion: An active inference account of interoception and categorization."

3 There are cultural complexities to this learning. For example, girls tend to learn that it's okay to display and communicate sadness. Anger, not so much. For boys, it's the reverse.

4 Johnston, Champeau, Hartwig, Helmer, Komar, Krueger, and McCarthy. *Engaging literate minds: Developing children's social, emotional, and intellectual lives, K-3.* p. 175.
    Based on Beck, McKeown, and Kucan, "Taking delight in words: Using oral language to build young children's vocabularies."

5 Johnston. *Opening minds: Using language to change lives.*

6 Roorda, Koomen, Spilt, and Oort. "The influence of affective teacher–student relationships on students' school engagement and achievement: A meta-analytic approach."

7 Johnston, Champeau, Hartwig, Helmer, Komar, Krueger, and McCarthy. *Engaging literate minds: Developing children's social, emotional, and intellectual lives, K-3.*

8 Mischel and Baker. "Cognitive appraisals and transformations in delay behavior."
    Moore, Mischel, and Zeiss. "Comparative effects of the reward stimulus and its cognitive representation in voluntary delay."

9 Haimovitz, Dweck, and Walton. "Preschoolers find ways to resist temptation after learning that willpower can be energizing."

10 Blair and Razza. "Relating effortful control, executive function, and false belief understanding to emerging math and literacy ability in kindergarten."

Gestsdottir, von Suchodoletz, Wanless, Hubert, Guimard, Birgisdottir, Gunzenhauser, and McClelland. "Early behavioral self-regulation, academic achievement, and gender: Longitudinal findings from France, Germany, and Iceland."

Duckworth, Tsukayama, and Quinn. "What no child left behind leaves behind: The roles of IQ and self-control in predicting standardized achievement test scores and report card grades."

Duckworth and Seligman. "Self-discipline outdoes IQ in predicting academic performance of adolescents."

McClelland and Cameron. "Self-regulation and academic achievement in elementary school children."

11 Duckworth, Tsukayama, and Quinn. "What no child left behind leaves behind: The roles of IQ and self-control in predicting standardized achievement test scores and report card grades."

Duckworth and Seligman. "Self-discipline outdoes IQ in predicting academic performance of adolescents."

12 Blair and Razza. "Relating effortful control, executive function, and false belief understanding to emerging math and literacy ability in kindergarten."

Daly, Delaney, Egan, and Baumeister. "Childhood self-control and unemployment throughout the life span: Evidence from two British cohort studies."

Daly, Egan, Quigley, Delaney, and Baumeister. "Childhood self-control predicts smoking throughout life: Evidence from 21,000 cohort study participants."

Duckworth, Tsukayama, and Quinn. "What no child left behind leaves behind: The roles of IQ and self-control in predicting standardized achievement test scores and report card grades."

Eisenberg, Spinrad, Valiente, and Duckworth. "Conscientiousness: Origins in Childhood?"

Heckman, Stixrud, and Urzua. "The effects of cognitive and non-cognitive abilities on labor market outcomes and social behavior."

Moffitt, Arseneault, Belsky, Dickson, Hancox, Harrington, Houts, Poulton, Roberts, Ross, Sears, Murray Thomson, and Caspi. "A gradient of childhood self-control predicts health, wealth, and public safety."

McClelland et al. "Links between behavioral regulation and preschoolers' literacy, vocabulary, and math skills."

Valiente, Lemery-Chalfant, Swanson, and Reiser. "Prediction of children's academic competence from their effortful control, relationships, and classroom participation."

13 Moffitt, Arseneault, Belsky, Dickson, Hancox, Harrington, Houts, Poulton, Roberts, Ross, Sears, Murray Thomson, and Caspi. "A gradient of childhood self-control predicts health, wealth, and public safety."

14 Johnston. *Opening minds: Using language to change lives.*

15 Johnston. *Opening minds: Using language to change lives.* p. 76.

16 Koopman and Hakemulder. "Effects of literature on empathy and self-reflection: A theoretical-empirical framework."

17 Eder. "Comments on children's self-narratives."

18 Caillies and Le Sourn-Bissaoui. "Children's understanding of idioms and theory of mind development."

19 Johnston, Bennett, and Cronin. "Literate achievements in fourth grade." p. 201.

20 Wharton-McDonald and Williamson. "Focus on the real and make sure it connects to kids' lives." p. 80.

21 Ivey and Johnston. "Engagement with young adult literature: Outcomes and processes."

22 Johnston, Layden, and Powers. *Children's literate talk and relationships.* p. 20.

23 Pittinsky and Montoya. "Empathic joy in positive intergroup relations."

24 Hatfield, Cacioppo, and Rapson. *Emotional contagion.*

25 Frenzel, Becker-Kurz, Pekrun, Goetz, and Lüdtke. "Emotion transmission in the classroom revisited: A reciprocal effects model of teacher and student enjoyment."

Mainhard, Oudman, Hornstra, Bosker, and Goetz. "Student emotions in class: The relative importance of teachers and their interpersonal relations with students."

26 Ric. "Effects of the activation of affective information on stereotyping: When sadness increases stereotype use."

27 Ray and Glover. *Already ready: Nurturing writers in preschool and kindergarten.* p. 141.

In a read aloud, this brilliant teacher comment, beginning with a noticing, brings together much of what we have discussed. It invites children to think about others' thoughts and feelings on multiple levels. It draws attention to the details of facial expression in the illustration, deepening understanding of, and engagement with, the story, while expanding the accuracy of children's mind reading. The comments invite children to imagine the motivations not just of the character, but also of the illustrator, laying the groundwork for critical literacy while drawing attention to strategies children might use in their own compositions.

Chapter 8: Knowing

1 Palmer. *To know as we are known: Education as a spiritual journey.*
2 Nystrand, Gamoran, Kachur, and Prendergast. *Opening dialogue: Understanding the dynamics of language and learning in the English classroom.* p. 72, their italics.
3 Smith, Hardman, Wall, and Mroz. "Interactive whole class teaching in the National Literacy and Numeracy Strategies." p. 408. Only 10 per cent of teacher questions were open with the average student response lasting five seconds and limited to three words or fewer in 70 per cent of answers; 15 per cent of teachers asked no open questions.
4 Cazden. *Classroom discourse: The language of teaching and learning.*
  Coulthard. *Conversational analysis: An introduction to discourse analysis.*
5 See Wells. "The case for dialogic inquiry."
6 Johnston, Jiron, and Day. "Teaching and learning literate epistemologies." p. 226.
7 Alexander. "Developing dialogic teaching: Genesis, process, trial." p. 565.
8 Au and Mason. "Cultural congruence in classroom participation structures: Achieving a balance of rights."
  Lee. *Culture, literacy, and learning: Taking bloom in the midst of the whirlwind.*
  Philips. *The invisible culture: Communication in classroom and community on the Warm Springs Indian Reservation.*
9 Rogoff and Toma. "Shared thinking: Community and institutional variations."
10 Applebee. *Curriculum as conversation: Transforming traditions of teaching and learning.*
  Johnston, Jiron, and Day. "Teaching and learning literate epistemologies."
  Ladson-Billings. *The dreamkeepers: Successful teachers of African American children.*
  Nystrand, Gamoran, Kachur, and Prendergast. *Opening dialogue: Understanding the dynamics of language and learning in the English classroom.*
11 Murdoch, English, Hintz, and Tyson. "Feeling heard: Inclusive education, transformative learning, and productive struggle."
12 Roorda, Koomen, Spilt, and Oort. "The influence of affective teacher–student relationships on students' school engagement and achievement: A meta-analytic approach."
  Lavy and Naama-Ghanayim. "Why care about caring? Linking teachers' caring and sense of meaning at work with students' self-esteem, well-being, and school engagement." n.p.

13 See Lindfors. *Children's inquiry: Using language to make sense of the world.*

14 Comeyras. "What can we learn from students' questions?"

15 Dillon. "The remedial status of student questioning."
   Nystrand, Gamoran, Kachur, and Prendergast. *Opening dialogue: Understanding the dynamics of language and learning in the English classroom.*

16 Allington. "Teacher interruption behaviors during primary-grade oral reading."

17 Carlsen. "Questioning in classrooms: A sociolinguistic perspective."
   Honea. "Wait time as an instructional variable: An influence on teacher and student."
   Fagan, Hassler, and Szabl. "Evaluation of questioning strategies in language arts instruction."

18 Johnston and Backer. "Inquiry and a good conversation: 'I learn a lot from them.'" p. 50.

19 Feldman and Wertsch. "Context dependent properties of teachers' speech."

20 Mercer. *Words and minds: How we use language to think together.*

21 Johnston, Champeau, Hartwig, Helmer, Komar, Krueger, and McCarthy. *Engaging literate minds: Developing children's social, emotional, and intellectual lives, K-3.*

22 Johnston and Backer. "Inquiry and a good conversation: 'I learn a lot from them.'" p. 42.

23 Cowhey. *Black ants and buddhists: Thinking critically and teaching differently in the primary grades.* p. 158

24 Johnston and Backer. "Inquiry and a good conversation: 'I learn a lot from them.'" p. 47.

25 Kuhn, Garcia-Mila, Zohar, and Anderson. *Strategies of knowledge acquisition.* p. 15.

26 Adams. *A descriptive study of second graders' conversations about books.* p. 137.

27 Johnston and Backer. "Inquiry and a good conversation: 'I learn a lot from them.'" p. 133.

28 Wharton-McDonald and Williamson. "Focus on the real and make sure it connects to kids' lives." p. 82.

29 Nystrand, Gamoran, Kachur, and Prendergast. *Opening dialogue: Understanding the dynamics of language and learning in the English classroom.*
   Wertsch, Tulviste, and Hagstrom. "A sociocultural approach to agency."

30 Nystrand, Gamoran, Kachur, and Prendergast. *Opening dialogue: Understanding the dynamics of language and learning in the English classroom.*

31 Smith, Hardman, Wall, and Mroz. "Interactive whole class teaching in the National Literacy and Numeracy Strategies."

Nystrand, Gamoran, Kachur, and Prendergast. *Opening dialogue: Understanding the dynamics of language and learning in the English classroom.*

32 Wells. *Dialogue and the development of the agentive individual: An educational perspective.* Wells. "The case for dialogic inquiry."

33 Lindfors. *Children's inquiry: Using language to make sense of the world.*

34 Miller. *Happy Reading. Tape 3.*

35 Department of Education Training and Employment. *Social action through literacy: Early to primary years.* University of South Australia.

Chapter 9: An Evolutionary, Democratic Learning Community

1 Greene. "The role of education in democracy." p. 3.

2 Pradl. "Reading and democracy: The enduring influence of Louise Rosenblatt." pp. 11–12.

3 Cacioppo, Hawkley, Norman, and Berntson. "Social isolation."

Immordino-Yang, Darling-Hammond, and Krone. "Nurturing nature: How brain development is inherently social and emotional, and what this means for education."

4 Immordino-Yang, Darling-Hammond, and Krone. "Nurturing nature: How brain development is inherently social and emotional, and what this means for education." p. 188.

5 Young. *Critical theory and classroom talk.* p. 8.

6 Rogoff and Toma. "Shared thinking: Community and institutional variations."

7 Rogoff and Toma. "Shared thinking: Community and institutional variations."

Young. *Critical theory and classroom talk.*

8 Nichols. *Talking about text: Guiding students to increase comprehension through purposeful talk.* p. 63.

9 Murdoch, English, Hintz, and Tyson. "Feeling heard: Inclusive education, transformative learning, and productive struggle."

10 Nichols. *Talking about text: Guiding students to increase comprehension through purposeful talk.* p. 89

11 Johnston. "Unpacking literate 'achievement.'" p. 35.

12 Johnston, Champeau, Hartwig, Helmer, Komar, Krueger, and McCarthy. *Engaging literate minds: Developing children's social, emotional, and intellectual lives, K-3.* p. 144.

13 Johnston, Champeau, Hartwig, Helmer, Komar, Krueger, and McCarthy. *Engaging literate minds: Developing children's social, emotional, and intellectual lives, K-3.* p. 144.

14 O'Connor and Michaels. "Supporting teachers in taking up productive talk moves: The long road to professional learning at scale."

15 Nichols. Talking about text: Guiding students to increase comprehension through purposeful talk. p. 64.

16 Troyer and Youngreen. "Conflict and creativity in groups."

17 Dong, Anderson, Il-Hee, and Yuan. "Collaborative reasoning in China and Korea."

18 Mercer, Wegerif, and Dawes. "Children's talk and the development of reasoning in the classroom."

19 Cazden. *Classroom discourse: The language of teaching and learning.*
   Nystrand, Gamoran, Kachur, and Prendergast. *Opening dialogue: Understanding the dynamics of language and learning in the English classroom.*

20 Rogoff and Toma. "Shared thinking: Community and institutional variations."

21 Mercer. *Words and minds: How we use language to think together.*

22 Doise and Mugny. *The social development of the intellect.*
   Schaffer. "Joint involvement episodes as context for development."

23 Miller. "Learning how to contradict and still pursue a common end— the ontogenesis of moral argumentation."

24 Barber. *Strong democracy: Participatory politics for a new age.*
   Burbules. *Dialogue in teaching: Theory and practice.*

25 Dyson. *Social worlds of children learning to write in an urban primary school.*

26 Johnston, Champeau, Hartwig, Helmer, Komar, Krueger, and McCarthy. *Engaging literate minds: Developing children's social, emotional, and intellectual lives, K-3.*

27 Johnston and Backer. "Inquiry and a good conversation: 'I learn a lot from them.'" p. 49.

28 Senge. *The fifth discipline: The art and practice of the learning organization.*

29 Barber. *Strong democracy: Participatory politics for a new age.*

30 Bovard. *Lost rights: The destruction of American liberty.* p. 333.

Chapter 10: Who Do You Think You're Talking To?

1 Smithyman (1972), cited in McQueen and Wedde. *The Penguin book of New Zealand verse.* p. 27.

2 Kingsolver. "Quality time." p. 68.

3 Mitchell. "Americans' talk to dogs: Similarities and differences with talk to infants."

4 Ivey and Johnston. *Teens choosing to read: Fostering social, emotional and intellectual growth through books.*

5 Nuamah and Mulroy. "'I am a child!': Public perceptions of Black girls and their punitive consequences."

6 Gee. *Social linguistics and literacies: Ideology in discourses.* p. 127

7 Johnston. "Unpacking literate 'achievement.'" p. 30.

8 Johnston, Jiron, and Day. "Teaching and learning literate epistemologies." pp. 225–226.

9 Johnston, Jiron, and Day. "Teaching and learning literate epistemologies." pp. 227–228.

10 Johnston, Bennett, and Cronin. "'I want students who are thinkers.'" p. 140.

11 Miller. *Happy Reading. Tape 3.*

12 Miller. *Happy Reading. Tape 1.*

13 Rio and Alvarez. "From activity to directivity: The question of involvement in education." pp. 59–83.

14 Johnston, Bennett, and Cronin. "'I want students who are thinkers.'" p. 149.

15 Young. *Critical theory and classroom talk.*

Appendix A

1 February 14, 1961, *The Wall Street Journal*, Pepper and Salt, page 12, column 6. https://quoteinvestigator.com/2021/06/08/small-print/#f+439731+1+1

2 Bourdieu. *The logic of practice.*

3 Wood, Bruner, and Ross. "The role of tutoring in problem solving." p. 92.

4 Scollon and Scollon. *Narrative, literacy, and face in interethnic communication.*

5 Ladson-Billings. *The dreamkeepers: Successful teachers of African American children.*

   Applebee. *Curriculum as conversation: Transforming traditions of teaching and learning.*

   Nystrand, Gamoran, Kachur, and Prendergast. *Opening dialogue: Understanding the dynamics of language and learning in the English classroom.*

6 Michaels. "Narrative presentations: An oral preparation for literacy with first grade."

7 Wortham. *Narratives in action: A strategy for research and analysis.*

8 In line with work by Bruner. "The 'remembered' self."

Dyson. "Coach Bombay's kids learn to write: Children's appropriation of media material for school literacy."

Harre. *The singular self: An introduction to the psychology of personhood.*

Wells. *Dialogue and the development of the agentive individual: An educational perspective.*

9 Bandura. "Self-efficacy: Toward a unifying theory of behavioral change."

10 Skinner, Zimmer-Gembeck, and Connell. *Individual differences and the development of perceived control.* p. 220.

11 Foote. "Attribution feedback in the elementary classroom." 155–166.

Licht. "Achievement-related belief in children with learning disabilities: Impact on motivation and strategy learning."

Nolen-Hoeksema, Girus, and Seligman. "Learned helplessness in children: A longitudinal study of depression, achievement, and explanatory style."

Skinner, Zimmer-Gembeck, and Connell. *Individual differences and the development of perceived control.* p. 220.

12 Grolnick and Ryan. "Parent styles associated with children's self-regulation and competence: A social contextual perspective."

Nolen-Hoeksema, Girus, and Seligman. "Learned helplessness in children: A longitudinal study of depression, achievement, and explanatory style."

13 Hokoda and Fincham. "Origins of children's helpless and mastery achievement patterns in the family."

Nowicki and Schneewind. "Relation of family climate variables to locus of control in German and American students."

Wagner and Phillips. "Beyond beliefs: Parent and child behaviors and children's perceived academic competence."

14 Gee. *Social linguistics and literacies: Ideology in discourses.* p. 127.

Appendix B

1 Johnston, Jiron, and Day. "Teaching and learning literate epistemologies."

References

Adam, H., & Galinsky, A.D. (2012). Enclothed cognition. *Journal of Experimental Social Psychology, 48*(4), 918–925. https://doi.org/10.1016/j.jesp.2012.02.008

Adams, E.L. (1995). *A descriptive study of second graders' conversations about books* [Doctoral dissertation, State University of New York at Albany].

Akinade, T., Kheyfets, A., Piverger, N., Layne, T.M., Howell, E.A., & Janevic, T. (2023). The influence of racial-ethnic discrimination on women's health care outcomes: A mixed methods systematic review. *Social Science & Medicine, 316*, n.p. https://doi.org/10.1016/j.socscimed.2022.114983

Alexander, R. (2018). Developing dialogic teaching: Genesis, process, trial. *Research Papers in Education, 33*(5), 561–598. https://doi.org/10.1080/02671522.2018.1481140

Allington, R.L. (1980). Teacher interruption behaviors during primary-grade oral reading. *Journal of Educational Psychology, 72*, 371–377.

Allington, R.L., & Johnston, P.H. (2002). Integrated instruction in exemplary fourth-grade classrooms. In R.L. Allington & P.H. Johnston (Eds.), *Reading to learn: Lessons from exemplary fourth-grade classrooms.* Guilford.

Allington, R.L., & Johnston, P.H. (Eds.). (2002). *Reading to learn: Lessons from exemplary fourth-grade classrooms.* Guilford.

Ambady, N., Shih, M., Kim, A., & Pittinsky, T.L. (2001). Stereotype susceptibility in children: Effects of identity activation on quantitative performance. *Psychological Science, 12*(5), 385–390.

Anderson, C. (2000). *How's it going: A practical guide to conferring with student writers.* Heinemann.

Applebee, A.N. (1996). *Curriculum as conversation: Transforming traditions of teaching and learning.* University of Chicago Press.

Aronson, J., Fried, C., & Good, C. (2002). Reducing the effects of stereotype threat on African American college students by shaping theories of intelligence. *Journal of Experimental Social Psychology, 38*, 113–125.

Au, K.H., & Mason, J.M. (1983). Cultural congruence in classroom participation structures: Achieving a balance of rights. *Discourse Processes*, 6, 145–167.

Austin, J. (1962). *How to do things with words*. Clarendon Press.

Baer, A.R., Grant, H., & Dweck, C.S. (2005). *Personal goals, dysphoria, & coping strategies*. Columbia University.

Bandura, A. (1977). Self-efficacy: Toward a unifying theory of behavioral change. *Psychological Review, 84*, 191–215.

Barber, B. (1984). *Strong democracy: Participatory politics for a new age*. University of California Press.

Baron, A.S. (2015). Constraints on the development of implicit intergroup attitudes. *Child Development Perspectives, 9*(1), 50–54. https://doi.org/10.1111/cdep.12105

Barrett, L.F. (2017). The theory of constructed emotion: An active inference account of interoception and categorization. *Social Cognitive & Affective Neuroscience, 12*(1), 1–23. https://doi.org/10.1093/scan/nsw154

Barrett, L.F. (2018). *How emotions are made: The secret life of the brain*. Houghton Mifflin.

Bateson, G. (1979). *Mind and nature: A necessary unity* (1st ed.). Dutton.

Beach, K. (1995). Activity as a mediator of sociocultural change and individual development: The case of school-work transition. *Mind, Culture and Activity, 2*, 285–302.

Beck, I.L., McKeown, M.G., & Kucan, L. (2003). Taking delight in words: Using oral language to build young children's vocabularies. *American Educator, 27*(1), 36–39, 41, 45–46.

Blair, C., & Razza, R.P. (2007). Relating effortful control, executive function, and false belief understanding to emerging math and literacy ability in kindergarten. *Child Development, 78*(2), 647–663. https://doi.org/10.1111/j.1467-8624.2007.01019.x

Bourdieu, P. (1990). *The logic of practice*. Polity Press.

Bovard, J. (1995). *Lost rights: The destruction of American liberty*. Palgrave MacMillan.

Brashares, A. (2003). *The second summer of the sisterhood*. Delacorte.

Brummelman, E., Thomaes, S., de Castro, B.O., Overbeek, G., & Bushman, B.J. (2014). "That's not just beautiful; that's incredibly beautiful!": The adverse impact of inflated praise on children with low self-esteem. *Psychological Science, 25*(3), 728–735. www.jstor.org.libproxy.albany.edu/stable/24540133

Bruner, J. (1994a). Life as narrative. In A.H. Dyson & C. Genishi (Eds.), *The need for story: Cultural diversity in classroom and community* (pp. 28–37). National Council of Teachers of English.

Bruner, J. (1994b). The "remembered" self. In U. Neisser & R. Fivush (Eds.), *The remembering self: Construction and accuracy in the self-narrative* (pp. 41–54). Cambridge University Press.

Burbules, N. (1993). *Dialogue in teaching: Theory and practice.* Teachers College Press.

Cacioppo, J.T., Hawkley, L.C., Norman, G.J., & Berntson, G.G. (2011). Social isolation. *Annals of the New York Academy of Sciences, 1231*(1), 17–22. https://doi.org/10.1111/j.1749-6632.2011.06028.x

Caillies, S., & Le Sourn-Bissaoui, S. (2008). Children's understanding of idioms and theory of mind development. *Developmental Science, 11*(5), 703–711. https://doi.org/10.1111/j.1467-7687.2008.00720.x

Caliskan, A., & Lewis, M. (2020). Social biases in word embeddings and their relation to human cognition. *PsyArXiv.* https://doi.org/10.31234/osf.io/d84kg

Campbell, T. (2015). Stereotyped at seven? Biases in teacher judgement of pupils' ability and attainment. *Journal of Social Policy, 44*(3), 517–547. https://doi.org/10.1017/S0047279415000227

Carlsen, W.S. (1991). Questioning in classrooms: A sociolinguistic perspective. *Review of Educational Research, 61,* 157–178.

Carr, P.B., Dweck, C.S., & Pauker, K. (2012). "Prejudiced" behavior without prejudice? Beliefs about the malleability of prejudice affect interracial interactions. *Journal of Personality & Social Psychology, 103*(3), 452–471. https://doi.org/10.1037/a0028849

Cazden, C. (2001). *Classroom discourse: The language of teaching and learning* (2nd ed.). Heinemann.

Cazden, C.B. (1992). Revealing and telling: The socialization of attention in learning to read and write. *Educational Psychology, 12,* 305–313.

Chang, D.F., & Sue, S. (2003). The effects of race and problem type on teachers' assessments of student behavior. *Journal of Consulting and Clinical Psychology, 71,* 235–242.

Charlesworth, T.E.S., Yang, V., Mann, T.C., Kurdi, B., & Banaji, M.R. (2021). Gender stereotypes in natural language: Word embeddings show robust consistency across child and adult language corpora of more than 65 million words. *Psychological Science, 32*(2), 218–240. https://doi.org/10.1177/0956797620963619

Cheng, J.T., Tracy, J.L., Kingstone, A., Foulsham, T., & Henrich, J. (2013). Two ways to the top: Evidence that dominance and prestige are distinct yet viable avenues to social rank and influence. *Journal of Personality & Social Psychology, 104*(1), 103–125. https://doi.org/10.1037/a0030398

Chiu, C., Dweck, C.S., Tong, J.Y., & Fu, J.H. (1997). Implicit theories and conceptions of morality. *Journal of Personality and Social Psychology, 3,* 923–940.

Cimpian, A., Arce, H.-M.C., Markman, E.M., & Dweck, C.S. (2007). Subtle linguistic cues affect children's motivation. *Psychological Science*, *18*(4), 314–316. https://doi.org/10.1111/j.1467-9280.2007.01896.x

Claro, S., Paunesku, D., & Dweck, C.S. (2016). Growth mindset tempers the effects of poverty on academic achievement. *Proceedings of the National Academy of Sciences: Psychological and Cognitive Sciences*, *113*(31), 8664–8668. https://doi.org/10.1073/pnas.1608207113

Clay, M. (1991). *Becoming literate: The construction of inner control.* Heinemann.

Clay, M.M. (1993). *Reading Recovery: A guidebook for teachers in training.* Heinemann.

Clay, M. (2001). *Change over time in children's literacy development.* Heinemann.

Comeyras, M. (1995). What can we learn from students' questions? *Theory Into Practice*, *34*(2), 101–106.

Coulthard, M. (1977). *Conversational analysis: An introduction to discourse analysis.* Longman.

Cowhey, M. (2006). *Black ants and buddhists: Thinking critically and teaching differently in the primary grades.* Stenhouse.

Crum, A.J., & Langer, E.J. (2007). Mind-set matters: Exercise and the placebo effect. *Psychological Science*, *18*(2), 165–171. https://doi.org/10.1111/j.1467-9280.2007.01867.x

Daly, M., Delaney, L., Egan, M., & Baumeister, R.F. (2015). Childhood self-control and unemployment throughout the life span: Evidence from two British cohort studies. *Psychological Science*, *26*(6), 709–723. https://doi.org/10.1177/0956797615569001

Daly, M., Egan, M., Quigley, J., Delaney, L., & Baumeister, R.F. (2016). Childhood self-control predicts smoking throughout life: Evidence from 21,000 cohort study participants. *Health Psychology*, *35*(11), 1254–1263. https://doi.org/10.1037/hea0000393

Darnon, C., Muller, D., Schrager, S.M., Pannuzzo, N., & Butera, F. (2006). Mastery and performance goals predict epistemic and relational conflict regulation. *Journal of Educational Psychology*, *98*(4), 766–776. https://doi.org/10.1037/0022-0663.98.4.766

Davies, B., & Harre, R. (1999). Positioning and personhood. In R. Harre & L. v. Langenhove (Eds.), *Positioning theory: Moral contexts of intentional action* (pp. 32–52). Blackwell.

Delpit, L. (1988). The silenced dialogue: Power and pedagogy in educating other people's children. *Harvard Educational Review*, *58*(3), 280–298.

Department of Education Training and Employment. (2000). *Social action through literacy: Early to primary years.* University of South Australia.

Dillon, J.T. (1988). The remedial status of student questioning. *Curriculum Studies*, *20*, 197–210.

Doise, W., & Mugny, G. (1984). *The social development of the intellect.* Pergamon Press.

Donaldson, M. (1978). *Children's minds.* W.W. Norton and Company.

Dong, T., Anderson, R.C., Il-Hee, K., & Yuan, L. (2008). Collaborative reasoning in China and Korea. *Reading Research Quarterly, 43*(4), 400–424. http://search.ebscohost.com/login.aspx?direct=true&db=a9h&AN=34693466&site=ehost-live

Duckworth, A.L., & Seligman, M.E.P. (2005). Self-discipline outdoes IQ in predicting academic performance of adolescents. *Psychological Science, 16*(12), 939–944. https://doi.org/10.1111/j.1467-9280.2005.01641.x

Duckworth, A.L., Tsukayama, E., & Quinn, P.D. (2012). What no child left behind leaves behind: The roles of IQ and self-control in predicting standardized achievement test scores and report card grades. *Journal of Educational Psychology, 104*(2), 439–451. https://doi.org/10.1037/a0026280

Dunham, P.J., Dunham, F., & Curwin, A. (1993). Joint-attentional states and lexical acquisition at 18 months. *Developmental Psychology, 29*, 827–831.

Dweck, C.S. (2000). *Self-theories: Their role in motivation, personality, and development.* Psychology Press.

Dyson, A.H. (1993). *Social worlds of children learning to write in an urban primary school.* Teachers College Press.

Dyson, A.H. (1999). Coach Bombay's kids learn to write: Children's appropriation of media material for school literacy. *Research in the Teaching of English, 33*(4), 367–402.

Dyson, A.H., & Genishi, C. (1994). Introduction: The need for story. In A.H. Dyson & C. Genishi (Eds.), *The need for story: Cultural diversity in classroom and community* (pp. 1–7). National Council of Teachers of English.

Eder, R.A. (1994). Comments on children's self-narratives. In U. Neisser & R. Fivush (Eds.), *The remembering self: Construction and accuracy in the self-narrative* (pp. 180–190). Cambridge University Press.

Eisenberg, N., Spinrad, T.L., Valiente, C., & Duckworth, A.L. (2014). Conscientiousness: Origins in childhood? *Developmental Psychology, 50*(5), 1331–1349. https://doi.org/10.1037/a0030977

Elbers, E., & Streefland, L. (2000). "Shall we be researchers again?" Identity and social interaction in a community of inquiry. In H. Cowie & G. v. d. Aalsvoort (Eds.), *Social interaction in learning and instruction: The meaning of discourse for the construction of knowledge* (pp. 35–51). Pergamon Press.

Fagan, E.R., Hassler, D.M., & Szabl, M. (1981). Evaluation of questioning strategies in language arts instruction. *Research in the Teaching of English, 15*, 267–273.

Feldman, C., & Wertsch, J. (1976). Context dependent properties of teachers' speech. *Youth and Society, 8*, 227–258.

Feldman, R. (2003). Infant–mother and infant–father synchrony: The coregulation of positive arousal. *Infant Mental Health Journal, 24*(1), 1–23. https://doi.org/10.1002/imhj.10041

FitzGerald, C., Martin, A., Berner, D., & Hurst, S. (2018). Interventions designed to reduce implicit prejudices and implicit stereotypes in real world contexts: A systematic review. *BMC Psychology, 7*, Article 29. https://doi.org/10.1186/s40359-019-0299-7

Fivush, R. (1994). Constructing narrative, emotion, and self in parent-child conversations about the past. In U. Neisser & R. Fivush (Eds.), *The remembering self: Construction and accuracy in the self-narrative* (pp. 136–157). Cambridge University Press.

Foote, C.J. (1999). Attribution feedback in the elementary classroom. *Journal of Research in Childhood Education, 13*(3), 155–166.

Frenzel, A.C., Becker-Kurz, B., Pekrun, R., Goetz, T., & Lüdtke, O. (2018). Emotion transmission in the classroom revisited: A reciprocal effects model of teacher and student enjoyment. *Journal of Educational Psychology, 110*(5), 628–639. https://doi.org/10.1037/edu0000228

Garg, N., Schiebinger, L., Jurafsky, D., & Zou, J. (2018). Word embeddings quantify 100 years of gender and ethnic stereotypes. *Proceedings of the National Academy of Sciences of the United States of America, 115*(16), E3635–E3644. https://doi.org/10.1073/pnas.1720347115

Gauvain, M. (2001). *The social context of cognitive development.* Guilford.

Gee, E., & Gee, J.P. (2017). Games as distributed teaching and learning systems. *Teachers College Record, 119*(12), 1–22. https://doi.org/10.1177/016146811711901202

Gee, J.P. (1996). *Social linguistics and literacies: Ideology in discourses* (2nd ed.). Falmer Press.

Gestsdottir, S., von Suchodoletz, A., Wanless, S., Hubert, B., Guimard, P., Birgisdottir, F., Gunzenhauser, C., & McClelland, M. (2014). Early behavioral self-regulation, academic achievement, and gender: Longitudinal findings from France, Germany, and Iceland. *Applied Developmental Science, 18*(2), 90–109. https://doi.org/10.1080/10888691.2014.894870

Graves, D.H. (1994). *A fresh look at writing.* Heinemann.

Greene, M. (1985). The role of education in democracy. *Educational Horizons, 63*, 3–9.

Grice, H.P. (1975). Logic and conversation. In P. Cole & J.L. Morgan (Eds.), *Syntax and semantics 3: Speech acts* (pp. 41–58). Academic Press.

Grolnick, W.S., & Ryan, R.M. (1989). Parent styles associated with children's self-regulation and competence: A social contextual perspective. *Journal of Educational Psychology, 81*, 143–154.

Guthrie, J.T., & Humenick, N.M. (2004). Motivating students to read: Evidence for classroom practices that increase reading motivation and achievement. In P.M.V. Chhabra (Ed.), *The voice of evidence in reading research* (pp. 329–354). Brookes.

Haimovitz, K., & Dweck, C.S. (2016). What predicts children's fixed and growth intelligence mind-sets? Not their parents' views of intelligence but their parents' views of failure. *Psychological Science, 27*(6), 859–869. https://doi.org/10.1177/0956797616639727

Haimovitz, K., & Dweck, C.S. (2017). The origins of children's growth and fixed mindsets: New research and a new proposal. *Child Development, 88*(6), 1849–1859. https://doi.org/10.1111/cdev.12955

Haimovitz, K., Dweck, C.S., & Walton, G.M. (2020). Preschoolers find ways to resist temptation after learning that willpower can be energizing. *Developmental Science, 23*(3), 1–10. https://doi.org/10.1111/desc.12905

Haimovitz, K.K., Kratzer, M.L., Kenthirarajah, D., Walton, G., & Dweck, C.S. (2016). *The power of "yet": Communicating the potential to improve through subtle cues in feedback.* Stanford University.

Halliday, M.A.K. (1993). Towards a language-based theory of learning. *Linguistics and Education, 5,* 93–116.

Halliday, M.A.K. (1994). *An introduction to functional grammar* (2nd ed.). Edward Arnold.

Harre, R. (1998). *The singular self: An introduction to the psychology of personhood.* Sage.

Harre, R., & Gillet, G. (1994). *The discursive mind.* Sage.

Hatfield, E., Cacioppo, J.T., & Rapson, R.L. (1994). *Emotional contagion.* Cambridge University Press.

Hauser, D.J., & Schwarz, N. (2022). Implicit bias reflects the company that words keep. *Frontiers in Psychology, 13,* 871221. https://doi.org/10.3389/fpsyg.2022.871221

Heckman, J.J., Stixrud, J., & Urzua, S. (2006). The effects of cognitive and noncognitive abilities on labor market outcomes and social behavior. *Journal of Labor Economics, 24*(3), 411–482. https://doi.org/10.1086/504455

Hokoda, A., & Fincham, F.D. (1995). Origins of children's helpless and mastery achievement patterns in the family. *Journal of Educational Psychology, 87,* 375–385.

Honea, M. (1982). Wait time as an instructional variable: An influence on teacher and student. *Clearinghouse, 56,* 167–170.

Hong, Y.-Y., Chiu, C.-Y., Dweck, C.S., Lin, D.M.-S., & Wan, W. (1999). Implicit theories, attributions, and coping: A meaning system approach. *Journal of Personality and Social Psychology, 77*(3), 588–599. https://www.academia.edu/12313698/Implicit_theories_attributions_and_coping_A_meaning_system_approach

Hooper, S.Y., Haimovitz, K., Wright, C., Murphy, M., & Yeager, D.S. (2016). *Creating a classroom incremental theory matters, but it's not as straightforward as you might think: Evidence from a multi-level analysis at ten high schools.* Society for Research on Adolescence.

Horn, M., & Giacobbe, M.E. (2007). *Talking, drawing, writing: Lessons for our youngest writers.* Stenhouse.

Immordino-Yang, M.H., Darling-Hammond, L., & Krone, C.R. (2019). Nurturing nature: How brain development is inherently social and emotional, and what this means for education. *Educational Psychologist, 54*(3), 185–204. https://doi.org/10.1080/00461520.2019.1633924

Immordino-Yang, M.H., & Gotlieb, R. (2017). Embodied brains, social minds, cultural meaning: Integrating neuroscientific and educational research on social-affective development. *American Educational Research Journal, 54*(1, suppl), 344S–367S. https://doi.org/10.3102/0002831216669780

Ivey, G. (2002). "Responsibility and respect for themselves and for whatever it is they're doing": Learning to be literate in an inclusion classroom. In R.L. Allington & P.H. Johnston (Eds.), *Reading to learn: Lessons from exemplary fourth-grade classrooms* (pp. 54–77). Guilford Press.

Ivey, G., & Broaddus, K. (2001). "Just plain reading": A survey of what makes students want to read in middle school classrooms. *Reading Research Quarterly, 36*(4), 350. http://search.ebscohost.com/login.aspx?direct=true&db=a9h&AN=5436223&site=ehost-live

Ivey, G., & Johnston, P. (2023). *Teens choosing to read: Fostering social, emotional and intellectual growth through books.* Teachers College Press.

Ivey, G., & Johnston, P.H. (2013). Engagement with young adult literature: Outcomes and processes. *Reading Research Quarterly, 48*(3), 255–275.

Ivey, G., Johnston, P.H., & Cronin, J. (1998). *Process talk and children's sense of literate competence and agency.* n.p.

Johnston, P., Champeau, K., Hartwig, A., Helmer, S., Komar, M., Krueger, T., & McCarthy, L. (2020). *Engaging literate minds: Developing children's social, emotional, and intellectual lives, K-3.* Stenhouse.

Johnston, P.H. (1999). Unpacking literate "achievement." In J. Gaffney & B. Askew (Eds.), *Stirring the waters: A tribute to Marie Clay* (pp. 27–46). Heinemann.

Johnston, P.H. (2012). *Opening minds: Using language to change lives.* Stenhouse.

Johnston, P.H., & Backer, J. (2002). Inquiry and a good conversation: "I learn a lot from them." In R.L. Allington & P.H. Johnston (Eds.), *Reading to learn: Lessons from exemplary fourth-grade classrooms* (pp. 37–53). Guilford.

Johnston, P.H., Bennett, T., & Cronin, J. (2002a). "I want students who are thinkers." In R.L. Allington & P.H. Johnston (Eds.), *Reading to learn: Lessons from exemplary fourth-grade classrooms* (pp. 140–165). Guilford.

Johnston, P.H., Bennett, T., & Cronin, J. (2002b). Literate achievements in fourth grade. In R.L. Allington & P.H. Johnston (Eds.), *Reading to learn: Lessons from exemplary fourth-grade classrooms* (pp. 188–203). Guilford Press.

Johnston, P.H., Guice, S., Baker, K., Malone, J., & Michelson, N. (1995). Assessment of teaching and learning in "literature based" classrooms. *Teaching and Teacher Education, 11*(4), 359–371.

Johnston, P.H., & Ivey, G. (2016). Classroom talk and individual differences in reading. In P. Afflerbach (Ed.), *Handbook of individual differences in reading: Text and context* (pp. 209–222). Routledge.

Johnston, P.H., Jiron, H.W., & Day, J.P. (2001). Teaching and learning literate epistemologies. *Journal of Educational Psychology, 93*(1), 223–233.

Johnston, P.H., Layden, S., & Powers, S. (1999). *Children's literate talk and relationships.* n.p.

Kamins, M.L., & Dweck, C.S. (1999). Person versus process praise and criticism: Implications for contingent self-worth and coping. *Developmental Psychology J1—Developmental Psychology, 35*(3), 835–847. http://search.epnet.com/login.aspx?direct=true&db=aph&an=1986834

Kay, M.R. (2018). *Not light, but fire: How to lead meaningful race conversations in the classroom.* Stenhouse.

Kay, M.R., & Orr, J. (2023). *We're gonna keep on talking: How to lead meaningful race conversations in the elementary classroom.* Stenhouse.

Kelly, D.J., Quinn, P.C., Slater, A.M., Lee, K., Gibson, A., Smith, M., Ge, L., & Pascalis, O. (2005). Three-month-olds, but not newborns, prefer own-race faces. *Developmental Science, 8*(6), F31–F36. https://doi.org/10.1111/j.1467-7687.2005.0434a.x

Kingsolver, B. (1989). Quality time. In B. Kingsolver (Ed.), *Homeland and other stories* (pp. 64–76). HarperCollins.

Koch, S., Pascalis, L., Vivian, F., Meurer Renner, A., Murray, L., & Arteche, A. (2019). Effects of male postpartum depression on father–infant interaction: The mediating role of face processing. *Infant Mental Health Journal, 40*(2), 263–276. https://doi.org/10.1002/imhj.21769

Kondo, D.K. (1990). *Crafting selves: Power, gender, and discourses of identity in a Japanese workplace.* University of Chicago Press.

Koopman, E.M., & Hakemulder, F. (2015). Effects of literature on empathy and self-reflection: A theoretical-empirical framework. *Journal of Literary Theory, 9*(1), 79–111. https://doi.org/10.1515/jlt-2015-0005

Kuhn, D., Garcia-Mila, M., Zohar, A., & Anderson, C. (1995). *Strategies of knowledge acquisition* (Vol. 60, No. 4). Monographs of the Society for Research in Child Development.

Ladson-Billings, G. (1994). *The dreamkeepers: Successful teachers of African American children.* Jossey-Bass.

Langenhove, L. v., & Harre, R. (1999). Introducing positioning theory. In R. Harre & L. v. Langenhove (Eds.), *Positioning theory: Moral contexts of intentional action* (pp. 14–31). Blackwell.

Langer, E. (1989). *Mindfulness.* Addison-Wesley.

Langer, E. (1997). *The power of mindful learning.* Addison-Wesley.

Langer, E.J., & Piper, A.I. (1987). The prevention of mindlessness. *Journal of Personality and Social Psychology, 53*(2), 280–287.

Lavy, S., & Naama-Ghanayim, E. (2020). Why care about caring? Linking teachers' caring and sense of meaning at work with students' self-esteem, well-being, and school engagement. *Teaching & Teacher Education, 91*, n.p. https://doi.org/10.1016/j.tate.2020.103046

Lee, C.D. (2007). *Culture, literacy, and learning: Taking bloom in the midst of the whirlwind.* Teachers College Press.

Lee, H.Y., & Yeager, D.S. (2020). Adolescents with an entity theory of personality are more vigilant to social status and use relational aggression to maintain social status. *Social Development, 29*(1), 273–289. https://doi.org/10.1111/sode.12393

Levy, S.R., Plaks, J.E., Hong, Y.-Y., Chiu, C.-Y., & Dweck, C.S. (2001). Static versus dynamic theories and the perception of groups: Different routes to different destinations. *Personality & Social Psychology Review, 5*(2), 156–168. http://search.epnet.com/login.aspx?direct=true&db=aph&an=4802758

Levy-Tossman, I., Kaplan, A., & Assor, A. (2007). Academic goal orientations, multiple goal profiles, and friendship intimacy among early adolescents. *Contemporary Educational Psychology, 32*(2), 231–252. https://doi.org/10.1016/j.cedpsych.2006.06.001

Lewis, M., Cooper Borkenhagen, M., Converse, E., Lupyan, G., & Seidenberg, M.S. (2022). What might books be teaching young children about gender? *Psychological Science, 33*(1), 33–47. https://doi.org/10.1177/09567976211024643

Licht, B. (1993). Achievement-related belief in children with learning disabilities: Impact on motivation and strategy learning. In L.J. Meltzer (Ed.), *Strategy assessment and instruction for students with learning disabilities* (pp. 247–270). Pro-Ed.

Lindfors, J.W. (1999). *Children's inquiry: Using language to make sense of the world.* Teachers College Press.

Luria, A.R. (1973). *The working brain* (B. Haigh, Trans.). Penguin.

Lyons, C.A., Pinnell, G.S., & DeFord, D.E. (1993). *Partners in learning: Teachers and children in reading recovery.* Teachers College Press.

Mainhard, T., Oudman, S., Hornstra, L., Bosker, R.J., & Goetz, T. (2018). Student emotions in class: The relative importance of teachers and their interpersonal relations with students. *Learning & Instruction, 53*, 109–119. https://doi.org/10.1016/j.learninstruc.2017.07.011

McClelland, M.M., et al. (2007). Links between behavioral regulation and preschoolers' literacy, vocabulary, and math skills. *Developmental Psychology, 43*(4), 947–959.

McClelland, M.M., & Cameron, C.E. (2011). Self-regulation and academic achievement in elementary school children. *New Directions for Child & Adolescent Development, 2011*(133), 29–44. https://doi.org/10.1002/cd.302

McGinty, A.S., Justice, L.M., Piasta, S.B., Kaderavek, J., & Fan, X. (2012). Does context matter? Explicit print instruction during reading varies in its influence by child and classroom factors. *Early Childhood Research Quarterly, 27*(1), 77–89. https://doi.org/10.1016/j.ecresq.2011.05.002

McKinley, C., & Byrne, M.G. (2002). *One smile*. Illumination Arts.

McQueen, H., & Wedde, I. (Eds.). (1985). *The Penguin book of New Zealand verse*. Penguin.

Mercer, N. (2000). *Words and minds: How we use language to think together*. Routledge.

Mercer, N., Wegerif, R., & Dawes, L. (1999). Children's talk and the development of reasoning in the classroom. *British Educational Research Journal, 25*(1), 95–111. http://search.ebscohost.com/login.aspx?direct=true&db=aph&AN=1784491&site=ehost-live

Michael, A. (2014). *Raising race questions: Whiteness and inquiry in education*. Teachers College Press.

Michaels, S. (1986). Narrative presentations: An oral preparation for literacy with first grade. In J. Cook-Gumperz (Ed.), *The social construction of literacy* (pp. 94–116). Cambridge University Press.

Miele, D.B., & Molden, D.C. (2010). Naive theories of intelligence and the role of processing fluency in perceived comprehension. *Journal of Experimental Psychology: General, 139*, 535–557. https://doi.org/10.1037/a0019745

Miller, D. (2002a). *Happy Reading. Tape 1: Essentials: Tone, structure, and routines for creating and sustaining a learning community* [Videotape]. Stenhouse.

Miller, D. (2002b). *Happy Reading. Tape 3: Wise choices: Independence and instruction in book choice* [Videotape]. Stenhouse.

Miller, M. (1986). Learning how to contradict and still pursue a common end—the ontogenesis of moral argumentation. In J.C.-G. et al. (Eds.), *Children's worlds and children's language*. Mouton de Gruyter.

Mischel, W., & Baker, N. (1975). Cognitive appraisals and transformations in delay behavior. *Journal of Personality and Social Psychology, 31*(2), 254–261. https://doi.org/10.1037/h0076272

Mitchell, R.W. (2001). Americans' talk to dogs: Similarities and differences with talk to infants. *Research on Language and Social Interaction, 34*(2), 183–210.

Moffitt, T.E., Arseneault, L., Belsky, D., Dickson, N., Hancox, R.J., Harrington, H., Houts, R., Poulton, R., Roberts, B.W., Ross, S., Sears, M.R., Murray Thomson, W., & Caspi, A. (2011). A gradient of child-hood self-control predicts health, wealth, and public safety. *Proceedings of the National Academy of Sciences of the United States of America, 108*(7), 2693–2698. https://doi.org/10.1073/pnas.1010076108

Molden, D.C., & Dweck, C.S. (2006). Finding "meaning" in psychology. *American Psychologist, 61*(3), 192–203. https://doi.org/10.1037/0003-066X.61.3.192

Moll, L.C. (2019). Elaborating funds of knowledge: Community-oriented practices in international contexts. *Literacy Research: Theory, Method, and Practice, 68*(1), 130–138.

Moore, B., Mischel, W., & Zeiss, A. (1976). Comparative effects of the reward stimulus and its cognitive representation in voluntary delay. *Journal of Personality and Social Psychology, 34*(3), 419–424. https://doi.org/10.1037/0022-3514.34.3.419

Mueller, C. M., & Dweck, C. S. (1998). Praise for intelligence can undermine children's motivation and performance. *Journal of Personality and Social Psychology, 75*(1), 33–52. HYPERLINK "https://protect-us.mimecast.com/s/se8nC82o95fOVMWnPUnYQOd?domain=sciencedirect.com"http://www.sciencedirect.com/science/article/B6X01-46P4M6Y-1J/2/a9a2c7a75d4689a26befad86f4c61ad1

Murdoch, D., English, A.R., Hintz, A., & Tyson, K. (2020). Feeling heard: Inclusive education, transformative learning, and productive struggle. *Educational Theory, 70*(5), 653–679. https://doi.org/10.1111/edth.12449

Naraian, S. (2019). Teaching for "real": Reconciling explicit literacy instruction with inclusive pedagogy in a fourth-grade urban classroom. *Urban Education, 54*(10), 1581–1607. https://doi.org/10.1177/0042085916648742

National Center for Education Statistics. (2020). Race and ethnicity of public school teachers and their students. https://nces.ed.gov/pubs2020/2020103/index.asp

National Center on Disability and Journalism. (n.d.). Resources. https://ncdj.org/resources/

NEA Center for Social Justice. (2021). 7 harmful racial discourse practices to avoid. www.nea.org/professional-excellence/student-engagement/tools-tips/7-harmful-racial-discourse-practices-avoid

Neisser, U. (1976). *Cognition and reality: Principles and implications of cognitive psychology.* W.H. Freeman.

Nicholls, J.G. (1989). *The competitive ethos and democratic education.* Harvard University Press.

Nichols, M. (2008). *Talking about text: Guiding students to increase comprehension through purposeful talk*. Shell Education.

Nolen-Hoeksema, S., Girus, J.S., & Seligman, M.E.P. (1986). Learned helplessness in children: A longitudinal study of depression, achievement, and explanatory style. *Journal of Personality and Social Psychology, 51*, 435–442.

Nović, S. (2021). The harmful ableist language you unknowingly use. *BBC.* www.bbc.com/worklife/article/20210330-the-harmful-ableist-language-you-unknowingly-use

Nowicki, S., & Schneewind, K.A. (1982). Relation of family climate variables to locus of control in German and American students. *Journal of Genetic Psychology, 141*, 277–286.

Nuamah, S.A., & Mulroy, Q. (2023). "I am a Child!": Public perceptions of Black girls and their punitive consequences. *Journal of Race, Ethnicity & Politics, 8*(2), 182–201. https://doi.org/10.1017/rep.2023.13

Nussbaum, A.D., & Dweck, C.S. (2008). Defensiveness versus remediation: Self-theories and modes of self-esteem maintenance. *Personality and Social Psychology Bulletin, 34*, 599–612. https://doi.org/10.1177/0146167207312960

Nystrand, M., Gamoran, A., Kachur, R., & Prendergast, C. (1997). *Opening dialogue: Understanding the dynamics of language and learning in the English classroom*. Teachers College Press.

O'Connor, C., & Michaels, S. (2019). Supporting teachers in taking up productive talk moves: The long road to professional learning at scale. *International Journal of Educational Research, 97*, 166–175. https://doi.org/10.1016/j.ijer.2017.11.003

O'Reilley, M.R. (1993). *The peaceable classroom*. Boynton/Cook.

Paavola, L., Kunnari, S., & Moilanen, I. (2005). Maternal responsiveness and infant intentional communication: Implications for the early communicative and linguistic development. *Child: Care, Health & Development, 31*(6), 727–735. https://doi.org/10.1111/j.1365-2214.2005.00566.x

Palmer, P.J. (1993). *To know as we are known: Education as a spiritual journey*. HarperCollins.

Papandrea, M.T., Namazi, M., Ghanim, I., & Patten, S. (2023). Identifying racial and socioeconomic biases in New Jersey special education eligibility. *Language, Speech & Hearing Services in Schools, 54*(2), 600–617. https://doi.org/10.1044/2022_LSHSS-22-00138

Pearson, R.M., Melotti, R., Heron, J., Joinson, C., Stein, A., Ramchandani, P.G., & Evans, J. (2012). Disruption to the development of maternal responsiveness? The impact of prenatal depression on mother–infant interactions. *Infant Behavior & Development, 35*(4), 613–626. https://doi.org/10.1016/j.infbeh.2012.07.020

Philips, S.T. (1983). *The invisible culture: Communication in classroom and community on the Warm Springs Indian Reservation*. Longman.

Pinsker, J. (2018). The problem with "Hey guys." *The Atlantic*. www.theatlantic.com/family/archive/2018/08/guys-gender-neutral/568231/

Pittinsky, T.L., & Montoya, R.M. (2016). Empathic joy in positive intergroup relations. *Journal of Social Issues, 72*(3), 511–523. https://doi.org/10.1111/josi.12179

Pontecorvo, C., & Sterponi, L. (2002). Learning to argue and reason through discourse in educational settings. In G. Wells & G. Claxton (Eds.), *Learning for life in the 21st century: Sociocultural perspectives on the future of education* (pp. 127–140). Blackwell.

Porter, T., Catalán Molina, D., Cimpian, A., Roberts, S., Fredericks, A., Blackwell, L.S., & Trzesniewski, K. (2022). Growth-mindset intervention delivered by teachers boosts achievement in early adolescence. *Psychological Science, 33*(7), 1086–1096. https://doi.org/10.1177/09567976211061109

Pradl, G.M. (1996). Reading and democracy: The enduring influence of Louise Rosenblatt. *The New Advocate, 9*(1), 9–22.

Pressley, M., Allington, R.L., Wharton-MacDonald, R., Collins-Block, C., & Morrow, L. (2001). *Learning to read: Lessons from exemplary first-grade classrooms*. Guilford.

Pressley, M., & Woloshyn, V. (1995). *Cognitive strategy instruction that really improves children's academic performance* (2nd ed.). Brookline Books.

Rahman, L. (2019). *Disability language guide*. Stanford University. https://disability.stanford.edu/sites/g/files/sbiybj26391/files/media/file/disability-language-guide-stanford_1.pdf

Randall, W.L. (1995). *The stories we are*. University of Toronto Press.

Rattan, A., Good, C., & Dweck, C.S. (2012). "It's ok—Not everyone can be good at math": Instructors with an entity theory comfort (and demotivate) students. *Journal of Experimental Social Psychology, 48*(3), 731–737. https://doi.org/10.1016/j.jesp.2011.12.012

Ray, K.W. (1999). *Wondrous words: Writers and writing in the elementary classroom*. National Council of Teachers of English.

Ray, K.W., & Cleaveland, L. (2004). *About the authors: Writing workshops with our youngest writers*. Heinemann.

Ray, K.W., & Cleaveland, L. (2019). *A teachers' guide to getting started with beginning writers, K-2*. Heinemann.

Ray, K.W., & Glover, M. (2008). *Already ready: Nurturing writers in preschool and kindergarten*. Heinemann.

Reichenbach, R. (1998). The postmodern self and the problem of developing a democratic mind. *Theory and Research in Social Education, 26*(2), 226–237.

Repacholi, B. M. (1998). Infants' use of attentional cues to identify the referent of another person's emotional expression. *Developmental Psychology, 34*(5), 1017. https://doi.org/10.1037/0012-1649.34.5.1017

Ric, F. (2004). Effects of the activation of affective information on stereotyping: When sadness increases stereotype use. *Personality & Social Psychology Bulletin*, *30*(10), 1310–1321. https://doi.org/10.1177/0146167204264661

Riessman, C.K. (1993). *Narrative analysis* (Vol. 30). Sage.

Rio, P. d., & Alvarez, A. (2002). From activity to directivity: The question of involvement in education. In G. Wells & G. Claxton (Eds.), *Learning for life in the 21st century: Sociocultural perspectives on the future of education* (pp. 59–83). Blackwell.

Rittle-Johnson, B. (2006). Promoting transfer: Effects of self-explanation and direct instruction. *Child Development*, *77*(1), 1–15. https://doi.org/10.1111/j.1467-8624.2006.00852.x

Rogoff, B., & Toma, C. (1997). Shared thinking: Community and institutional variations. *Discourse Processes*, *23*(3), 471–497. https://doi.org/10.1080/01638539709545000

Roorda, D.L., Koomen, H.M.Y., Spilt, J.L., & Oort, F.J. (2011). The influence of affective teacher–student relationships on students' school engagement and achievement: A meta-analytic approach. *Review of Educational Research*, *81*(4), 493–529. https://doi.org/10.3102/0034654311421793

Schaffer, H.R. (1996). Joint involvement episodes as context for development. In H. Daniels (Ed.), *An introduction to Vygotsky* (pp. 251–280). Routledge.

Scollon, R. (1999). Mediated discourse and social interaction. *Research on Language & Social Interaction*, *32*(1/2), 149. http://search.ebscohost.com/login.aspx?direct=true&db=aph&AN=3344746&site=ehost-live

Scollon, R., & Scollon, S. (1981). *Narrative, literacy, and face in interethnic communication*. Ablex.

Seligman, M.E.P. (1975). *Helplessness: On depression, development, and death*. W.H. Freeman.

Senge, P.M. (1994). *The fifth discipline: The art and practice of the learning organization*. Doubleday.

Shannon, J.D., Tamis-LeMonda, C.S., & Cabrera, N.J. (2006). Fathering in infancy: Mutuality and stability between 8 and 16 months. *Parenting: Science & Practice*, *6*(2/3), 167–188. https://doi.org/10.1207/s15327922par0602&3_3

Shih, M., Wang, E., Bucher, A.T., & Stotzer, R. (2009). Perspective taking: Reducing prejudice towards general outgroups and specific individuals. *Group Processes & Intergroup Relations*, *12*(5), 565–577. https://doi.org/10.1177/1368430209337463

Skinner, E.A., Zimmer-Gembeck, M.J., & Connell, J.P. (1998). *Individual differences and the development of perceived control* (Vol. 63, No. 2–3). Monographs of the Society for Research in Child Development. https://doi.org/10.2307/1166220

Smith, F., Hardman, F., Wall, K., & Mroz, M. (2004). Interactive whole class teaching in the National Literacy and Numeracy Strategies. *British Educational Research Journal*, *30*(3), 395–411. https://doi.org/10.1080/0141192040100168970

Steele, C.M., & Aronson, J. (1995). Stereotype threat and the intellectual test performance of African Americans. *Journal of Personality & Social Psychology*, *69*(5), 797–811. http://search.ebscohost.com/login.aspx?direct=true&db=aph&AN=9512064011&site=ehost-live

Steig, W. (1976). *The amazing bone*. Puffin Books.

Stevenson, H. (2013). *Promoting racial literacy in schools: Differences that make a difference*. Teachers College Press.

Sun, J., Anderson, R.C., Lin, T.-J., Morris, J.A., Miller, B.W., Ma, S., Thi Nguyen-Jahiel, K., & Scott, T. (2022). Children's engagement during collaborative learning and direct instruction through the lens of participant structure. *Contemporary Educational Psychology*, *69*, 102061. https://doi.org/10.1016/j.cedpsych.2022.102061

Sun, K.L. (2015). *There's no limit: Mathematics teaching for a growth mindset* [Dissertation, Stanford University]. https://stacks.stanford.edu/file/druid:xf479cc2194/Sun-Dissertation-Upload-augmented.pdf

Sutton-Smith, B. (1995). Radicalizing childhood: The multivocal mind. In H. McEwan & K. Egan (Eds.), *Narrative in teaching, learning, and research* (pp. 69–90). Teachers College Press.

Taylor, B.M., Peterson, D.S., Pearson, P.D., & Rodriguez, M. (2002). Looking inside classrooms: Reflecting on the "how" as well as the "what" in effective reading instruction. *The Reading Teacher*, *56*, 70–79.

Tomasello, M., & Farrar, M.J. (1986). Joint attention and early language. *Child Development*, *57*(6), 1454–1463. https://www.jstor.org/stable/1130423

Tracy, J.L., & Robins, R.W. (2007). The psychological structure of pride: A tale of two facets. *Journal of Personality & Social Psychology*, *92*(3), 506–525. https://doi.org/10.1037/0022-3514.92.3.506

Troyer, L., & Youngreen, R. (2009). Conflict and creativity in groups. *Journal of Social Issues*, *65*(2), 409–427. doi:10.1111/j.1540-4560.2009.01606.x

Valiente, C., Lemery-Chalfant, K., Swanson, J., & Reiser, M. (2008). Prediction of children's academic competence from their effortful control, relationships, and classroom participation. *Journal of Educational Psychology*, *100*(1), 67–77. https://doi.org/10.1037/0022-0663.100.1.67

Vallotton, C.D. (2009). Do infants influence their quality of care? Infants' communicative gestures predict caregivers' responsiveness. *Infant Behavior & Development*, *32*(4), 351–365. https://doi.org/10.1016/j.infbeh.2009.06.001

Voina, A., & Stoica, M.S. (2023). Reframing leadership: Jacinda Ardern's response to the Covid-19 pandemic. *Media and Communications, 11*(1), 139–149.

Vygotsky, L.S. (1978). *Mind in society: The development of higher psychological processes.* Harvard University Press.

Wagner, B.M., & Phillips, D.A. (1992). Beyond beliefs: Parent and child behaviors and children's perceived academic competence. *Child Development, 63*, 1380–1391.

Wallis, C. (2021). Unequal surgery. *Scientific American, 325*(6), 30. https://libproxy.albany.edu/login?url=https://search.ebscohost.com/login.aspx?direct=true&AuthType=ip,sso&db=a9h&AN=153426230&site=ehost-live

Wells, G. (1998). *Dialogue and the development of the agentive individual: An educational perspective* [Symposium on "Human agency in cultural-historical approaches: Problems and perspectives"].

Wells, G. (2001). The case for dialogic inquiry. In G. Wells (Ed.), *Action, talk and text: Learning and teaching through inquiry* (pp. 171–194). Teachers College Press.

Wertsch, J.V., Tulviste, P., & Hagstrom, F. (1993). A sociocultural approach to agency. In E.A. Foorman, N. Minick, & C.A. Stone (Eds.), *Contexts for learning: Sociocultural dynamics in children's development* (pp. 336–356). Oxford University Press.

West, M.R., Buckley, K., Krachman, S.B., & Bookman, N. (2018). Development and implementation of student social-emotional surveys in the CORE districts. *Journal of Applied Developmental Psychology, 55*, 119–129.

Wharton-McDonald, R., Boothroyd, K., & Johnston, P. (1999). *Students' talk about readers and writers, reading and writing.* American Educational Research Association.

Wharton-McDonald, R., & Williamson, J. (2002). Focus on the real and make sure it connects to kids' lives. In R.L. Allington & P.H. Johnston (Eds.), *Reading to learn: Lessons from exemplary fourth-grade classrooms* (pp. 78–98). Guilford Press.

White, R.E., & Carlson, S.M. (2016). What would Batman do? Self-distancing improves executive function in young children. *Developmental Science, 19*(3), 419–426. https://doi.org/10.1111/desc.12314

White, R.E., Prager, E.O., Schaefer, C., Kross, E., Duckworth, A.L., & Carlson, S.M. (2017). The "Batman effect": Improving perseverance in young children. *Child Development, 88*(5), 1563–1571. https://doi.org/10.1111/cdev.12695

Williams, L.A., & Desteno, D. (2008). Pride and perseverance: The motivational role of pride. *Journal of Personality & Social Psychology, 94*(6), 1007–1017. https://doi.org/10.1037/0022-3514.94.6.1007

Wortham, S. (2001). *Narratives in action: A strategy for research and analysis.* Teachers College Press.

WVTM13. (2022). *Voters erase racist wording in Alabama Constitution.* www.wvtm13.com/article/alabama-constitution-slavery-racist-language/ 41848458#

Young, R. (1992). *Critical theory and classroom talk.* Multilingual Matters.

Zhu, S., & Wong, P.W.C. (2022). What matters for adolescent suicidality: Depressive symptoms or fixed mindsets? Examination of cross-sectional and longitudinal associations between fixed mindsets and suicidal ideation. *Suicide & Life-Threatening Behavior, 52*(5), 932–942. https:// doi.org/10.1111/sltb.12891

Index

Page numbers in **bold** denote a table. The letter n following a page number indicates a reference in the notes.